BREAK FREE

Unlock Your God Given Potential & Unleash Your Unstoppable

Ashley Winston

Linda,
God is good! He
keep seeking Him & He
will tell you what to do.
There is more!
Be Unstoppable!
Ashley

Ashley Winston

ISBN: 1986062023
ISBN-13: 978-1986062022

FOREWORD

Ashley Winston is known for her ability to inspire, motivate, and pull potential out of her audience, and in *BREAK FREE: Unlock Your God - Given Potential & Unleash Your Unstoppable,* she did not disappoint! This book is OUTSTANDING!

Whether you're an inquiring mind, curious about the tenants and precepts of Christianity, or you're a mature Christian, looking to be encouraged in your walk, and motivated to your next level of "unstoppable," this book is for you. We have never seen such a book that lends itself to such a wide span of Christian maturity. Another title for this book could have been "How to be an Awesome, Highly Productive Christian." Ashley takes us through the whole of the Christian walk: From the precepts of early Christianity, through discipleship – teaching us how to be a well-rounded believer – and then on to empowerment. After reading *Break Free,* you will truly know how to be a well-balanced Christian, who is not only powerful, but understands God's purpose for their life and knows how to empower others. The "Great Commission" given by Jesus Christ in Matthew 28:18-20 tells us to "go and make disciples..." This is exactly what Ashley does for us in this book, then empowers us to fulfill His plan by doing the same for others.

For the years that we have known Ashley, there are some key words that could most accurately describe her. One word that we would choose is FEARLESS. Over time, we have become acutely aware of Ashley's many skills and gifts, but what has impressed us the most is that she is not scared to step out and put those talents to work. Ashley's "get it done" attitude was put to the test when we asked her to step out of her comfort zone this past year. As we are over the youth ministry at our local church (Living Word Christian Center, Forest Park, IL), we have many people that volunteer to help us lead that charge. Ashley is one of those dedicated volunteers, giving her time to the teens and young adults, and the community. During our recent annual Freedom Conference (youth and young adult conference) we asked her to take on an important role that she did not necessarily ask for, but we knew she was the right person for the job. She did not have any formal training in this area, but her "get it done" attitude went right to work. She didn't complain, she didn't pout, and she didn't look for sympathy or a way out of it. She simply said, "Well, praise God." Her execution was nothing short of excellent in every way, and it showed. She knows what it feels like to be put in a position that releases your potential, even when it is uncomfortable. We have seen it happen inside of her over the years, resulting in Ashley's monumental growth.

This is what Ashley is all about – She never makes excuses; she just makes it happen. She lives out what she is writing about. She empowers others to break free. Ashley is incredibly strong-minded, diligent, loving, faithful, and positive – even in the midst of adverse conditions. This book is a pure reflection of Ashley's heart: unstoppable.

Pastor David & Niki Winston

CONTENTS

ACKNOWLEDGMENTS

To my Mom for her unconditional love, support, and for raising me to be the strong woman I am today.

For the memory of my Granddaddy whose witty words and wisdom guided me throughout the years, and who taught me that love is best expressed through giving.

To my Grandma Geri who always listens and believes in me. Her words of encouragement touch the innermost places of my heart in ways that words cannot express.

To my Sister-friend Adri for her expertise, tireless support, and countless hours of work. I would have never been able to write this book without her.

To my closest friends for showing up when they could have stayed home, encouraging me, and always pushing me towards purpose.

To my Pastor Dr. Bill Winston and my church family, Living Word Christian Center, for showing me what it means to live by faith. My life has never been the same.

PREFACE

I strongly dislike writing. I never thought I was a very good writer and like most people, I shied away from things I thought I couldn't conquer. So, when God told me to write a book, I was not thrilled. I had doubts and all the excuses: will anyone even read this book? I'm a terrible speller. How will I ever find the time to write 100,000 words? Growing up as a social butterfly, I knew that I could easily speak 100,000 words, but writing them down was a different story.

Isn't that how it goes with us and God sometimes? We try to disqualify ourselves from the very things that He is calling us to do. I believe that God is ready to do something amazing in your life. Whether you need to break free spiritually, financially, relationally, or emotionally - the opportunity is now. God's best is on the other side of your breakthrough. His best for your career, your church, your marriage, your business, your family, your future - it can all be found outside of your comfort zone and in the wild adventures of faith. I don't know what stage or season of life you're in, but I do know that no matter where you are, things can get better.

Unfortunately, many people never decide to push past their pain and into the fullness of God's promises. This reality bothers me. God is so good and He doesn't want us to live an ordinary, average, or mediocre life. He wants our lives to be extraordinary. He has placed so much possibility inside us. Through him we have access to unlimited potential, but the thing about potential is that it doesn't materialize without pressure. It requires the right set of circumstances and opportunities and it demands the right environment. I wrote this book to help you crack the code on your destiny lockbox. It's time to put an end to the insecurities and complacency that plague so many talented and gifted women and men. My desire is to see you become the person you were created to be, instead of dreaming about the person you are afraid to become. Whatever God has put in your heart to accomplish, it is possible. You probably already know this, but the real question is: do you believe it in your heart? Our actions tell on us. They show us what we truly believe.

Sometimes the hardest person to confront is ourselves - to really discover if we are being who we say we are. It's uncomfortable. It takes courage, but it is necessary for us to take inventory of where we are, so that we can move into where God is calling us. You were designed for greatness and to live from the inside out. One thing I've learned is that if I deal with what's happening inside of me, God will take care of what's happening around me.

We are all on our own individual and personal journey to unlock our full potential, purpose and destiny. We must learn to engage in the process of allowing God to build our character and deepen our capacity so that His plans and purposes can be revealed in our lives and in the Earth. We must learn to depend on God's wisdom to guide us, and His grace to carry us through.

Hear me out. Life will never stop happening to you or me. So, we must train ourselves to move forward while it happens. Believe in God. Believe in you.

The Love of A Father

My grandfather passed away a few years ago. He was the most influential person in my life. Leading up to the day of his funeral, I was so sad and nervous about how I would react to seeing him for the last time. Surprisingly, when the day came, I had this supernatural peace that was beyond my understanding. I wondered how it was possible. How could I feel such peace in the face of such loss, especially the loss of someone like my grandfather?

God comforted me in that moment. He reminded me that He gives us peace, even when peace seems not to be an option (John 14:27). Then, I started to reflect on the kind of relationship I had with my grandfather and all the memories we shared. We spent a lot of time together. I loved him very much, and I knew that he loved me.

His words and wisdom guided me in life. Our connection was full of love and support, and I was secure in the place I held in his heart, and while I was standing there, being reminded of all these wonderful attributes about my relationship with my grandfather, I realized that this was the kind of relationship that God desperately wanted to have with me - that He wants to have with all of us. I don't know what your relationship is like with your actual grandfather or father. You might have the greatest relationship in the world or you might not due to a divorce, death, or maybe he is physically present but just emotionally absent. Either way, I know that you have access to a heavenly father that will never leave you or forsake you. In those arms, you can always find refuge, unconditional love, support, direction, and true comfort and security, no matter what you are facing.

Most of you reading this book have never met my grandfather and never will, but through my relationship with him, you can know him. He lives in me through the memories we shared and the lessons he taught me. That is the power of relationship. It is only when we have an intimate, authentic connection with God that others will know Him.

So, who do people meet when they meet you. Do they meet God's wisdom? God's peace? Do they encounter the love of the Father?

CHAPTER 1

NAKED IN THE LIGHT

We must allow our true selves to be revealed, which can feel intimidating, overwhelming, and exhilarating all at the same time. That is the beginning of breaking free. Deciding in your heart, once and for all, not to play small anymore out of the fear of rejection or failing. This means not settling for anything less than God's absolute best in every area of your life. Being open and vulnerable takes courage, but God has wired us for genuine connections, and those are born out of our vulnerability. And vulnerability is the only way that we can experience the fullness of those connections and embrace who God is and who we are in our relationships with Him and others. Our connection with God, our purpose, and people are all threatened when we walk around wearing masks and self-protective shields. I understand that life can make you guarded, but I also understand the freedom that comes from really trusting God and developing intimacy in your relationship with Him.

There are many things that can make us live life guarded, like un-forgiveness, poor self-image, mistaken identity, sin, soul wounds, fear, and anxiety. You and I both know that the list could continue. But God wants us to live free from all of that. And the only way that can happen is if we are willing to lay down our protective shields and surrender. If we want to become all that God has called us to be and exhaust our potential on earth, we must first develop healthy relationships with ourselves and God.

I think about it like this; it's like we're in a "triangle."

Side note: I should warn you now. I have an undergraduate degree in theater. So, I'm expressive. I will probably use more exclamation points than most people think are appropriate (like my editor) and occasionally, I might say something totally random and challenge you to use your imagination. This is one of those times!

Ok, so back to the triangle! God is the top point, we are the bottom left corner, and the people in our lives are the bottom right. If we want our horizontal connections (you and others) to be healthy, then we should ensure that our vertical connection (you and God) is healthy. The quality of our lives will only reflect the quality of our personal relationship with God. We must be willing to let his light expose our hidden motives and agendas, but most importantly our treasure. We must allow God's truth to touch the most inner parts of our hearts so that we can be a light in the world.

In my twenties, I remember feeling like I was on an emotional roller coaster. Life had broken my heart in a variety of unexpected ways and it left me questioning myself. Am I enough for what I felt like God was calling me to do? I had already dealt with a lot by that point in my life. Making the transition from college student to a full-fledged adult was harder than expected. In college, I worked as the resident assistant in my dorm. It wasn't my favorite job, but it provided free housing. And that was awesome! But unfortunately, one of the conditions of my position as an RA was that I couldn't work another job. So, I didn't have any money when I graduated. Chicago is an expensive city to live in...especially when you are flat broke! Around that same time, I lost a relationship with a close friend who suddenly disappeared from my life. They got in some legal troubles and ran. I never saw them again. And on top of that, I was carrying around the weight of being sexually abused when I was younger. It had been years since it happened, but I never felt safe enough to share my secret with anyone except God. Like so many women and men, I didn't feel like I could share this deep and painful part of my past. Long story short - my life was a mess.

Normally, my go-getter nature and optimistic attitude would have been enough for me to rise above my feelings of insecurity and self-doubt. But this time it was different. I knew I needed something more and I found myself searching for it. My months of curiosity led me to a church. The same church I attend now.

It was there, where I learned about faith and what it meant to really have a relationship with God. It was also there, where I met Pastor Barbara. I was in a line coming out of a room with other people, who just like me had received baptism and decided to give their life to Christ. Pastor Barbara was in front of the door I had to walk through to get out of the room. She was smiling and hugging everyone. I remember standing there waiting for my turn when I felt prompted out of nowhere to tell her that I needed someone to talk to. I expressed a little more about what I had been going through and she invited me to meet with her a few weeks later. We met that week and then we started to meet every week after.

She became like a spiritual mother to me. Through our conversations, I could feel God healing the broken pieces of my heart. He was using her to teach me about vulnerability. He was using her to teach me how to "open up" again. I hated it and loved it all at the same time. Some days we laughed and other days there were tears. Pastor Barbara always had some sort of catchy, funny phrase to help me remember the essence of what we talked about when we were together. I don't know if she had been saying these phrases for years or if she was just making them up on the spot, but either way they were memorable and they stuck with me.

When I was not in her presence, her words would still ring true in my heart. One of these catchy phrases she would jokingly say to me was, "Remember Ashley... Naked in the Light". This saying was twofold. One, meaning, that you need to be comfortable with your body and in your own skin. That you need to be able to look at yourself in the mirror flaws and all and not only be "just okay" with what you see but love yourself and appreciate the way you were designed by God. You must be willing to accept all of you. Two, meaning, that you must be able to come to God spiritually "naked" when you are in His presence. This is just another way of saying that you need to come to God open and vulnerable. Bringing God all your baggage!

Thank God for Pastor Barbara. When I needed someone the most, especially when I wasn't sure how to handle the heartbreak, she was sent to me from God. He knew I needed some sort of guidance. She, along with the power of God, helped me see that I didn't need to isolate myself from the pain. Instead, I learned that I could give God my broken pieces and receive healing.

God loves you. He created you for His glory and His purposes. If you think about it, God made man in His image, and when He stepped back and looked at you as his finished work He called it good (Genesis 1:31). So, the next time you look in the mirror, look at yourself and say, "It's all good."

God wants you to come before Him spiritually naked. So, that He can cover you with His love. He knows everything you feel and the situations you've been through; He knows the challenges and setbacks that you've experienced. He knows the pain you've felt; and God wants to heal you. He wants you to let him into those secret places of your heart so that he can restore the broken pieces of your life. Don't worry, broken pieces don't scare God. In fact, your mess is the prerequisite for His masterpiece.

Think about it like this, in a friendship, if you don't reveal something that is bothering you or that you need help with, then that topic is never on the table for discussion. It is the same in your relationship with God. If you don't bring Him your secrets, there is not much room for intimacy. It's our willingness to be vulnerable that creates intimacy. Spending honest time with God is all we need to become whole. The more we are with Him, the more we become like Him.

Where Do You Start? Open Your Heart to God

There was a season in my life where my car would work fine with no issues for a certain period and then out of nowhere it would just stall on me. One day I parked my car to get coffee, came back out and tried to start it and it wouldn't work. It made a slight "zsst" noise like it was going to start but never did! This happened several times that day. The first time when I got coffee and then again when I stopped for lunch.

Anyway, I didn't have time to keep playing games with my car, so I called the auto shop and they told me to bring it in. I left my car with the mechanics hoping that they would be able to discover the problem but when I returned, they said there was nothing wrong with my car and that everything was working perfectly fine! How could this be? My car was starting and stopping all day and the mechanics claim it's perfectly fine. I was certain there was something wrong with it! I left the auto shop and eventually I experienced the same problem a few days later. I was leaving a store and when I came back my car wouldn't start, again! I took the car back to the auto shop, they put the car on the scanner and said once again that there was nothing wrong with it. They were looking at me like I was crazy. The mechanic told me that for the problem to be detected that my car had to stall at the actual auto shop. They needed it to malfunction and do whatever it was doing out there in the streets with me in front of them.

So, over a holiday weekend, I decided to leave my car in the shop. My thinking was surely if I leave the car with the mechanics for the weekend they will start the car and eventually it would go dead on them too. When I got back to town and entered the auto shop, yes you guessed it; they said my car was fine and that there was nothing wrong with it.

I couldn't believe it. At this point I was fed up. The mechanics told me to take the car back home because until it malfunctioned there, I was stuck with the problem. I walked back to my car discouraged. I did not want to risk driving it around anymore. Chicago winter was approaching, and I did not want my car to stall on me in the snow. I got in the car and turned the ignition. Guess what? Finally, the car would not start! I'd never been so happy to see that happen in my life.

I ran back into the auto shop and shouted, "It won't start! It won't start!" The mechanic came out, lifted the hood and he personally took out the battery. He hooked a scanner up to the car and inspected everything. After he tousled around with the battery and a few other things under the hood, he told me that the battery was faulty even though it looked perfect. He said, "the battery is showing up like it's fine but there's something causing it to leak." The defect was in the battery the whole time, but it was never detected until 1. The car malfunctioned at the auto shop and 2. The Mechanic could get under the hood.

The personal inspection allowed him to go directly where the problem was and fix it. He took the old battery out and gave me a brand new one. My car has been working perfectly fine ever since.

Moral of the story, you are the car and God is the mechanic. God cannot work on you the way he needs to if you show up "working perfectly fine" all the time. He needs you to be vulnerable enough to malfunction in His presence. He needs you to come to Him broken instead of you having it all together so that He can "look under your hood". Essentially, get into your heart and get to the root of your pain and or the problem. For you to live out the vision God has for your life, you must be willing to show up broken and to let God under your "hood". Let Him heal your heart and allow Him to detect the defects that have you on a "start-stop" journey. Let Him take out whatever is not working and replace it with what will. Let Him take out the old so he can give you the new. He loves you and He is waiting for you to enter into deeper fellowship with Him.

Psalm 51:10 New International Version (NIV)
Create in me a pure heart, O God,
and renew a steadfast spirit within me.

Psalm 10:17 New International Version (NIV)
You, Lord, hear the desire of the afflicted;
you encourage them, and you listen to their cry,

Psalm 139:23-24 New International Version (NIV)
Search me, God, and know my heart;
test me and know my anxious thoughts.
See if there is any offensive way in me,
and lead me in the way everlasting.

Showing up before God broken and naked is the beginning of you being able to commit yourself to the process of maturing in Christ. Let Him search you. The only way anything can be detected is if you allow yourself to be put through the scanner of Jesus Christ! The Holy Spirit!

John 16:13 New International Version (NIV)
13 But when he, the Spirit of truth, comes, he will guide you into all the truth. He will not speak on his own; he will speak only what he hears, and he will tell you what is yet to come.

When you get into God's presence, talk with Him; literally ask Him for help and to show you what is preventing you from being the full expression of the person He created you to be or from getting to that next level in your life. As you open up to God, He will begin to show you the truth. After He reveals it to you, no matter how hard it is to face, commit to the process of walking with Him as He continues to show you more about who He created you to be.

God loves when you come before Him broken because it shows Him that you understand your need (Psalm 51:17). God responds to need. There is nothing for Him to do, if we walk around like we have it all together. If you look at many of the stories in the Bible, God showed up when there was a need. When Jesus fed the 5,000, there was a need. In that story, the disciples didn't have enough food to feed everybody and they needed a solution (Matthew 14:13-21). When He healed the woman with the blood sickness, there was a need. She had been dealing with that infirmity for 12 years (Luke 8:40-47). When He healed the man at the pool of Bethesda, there was a need, the man was lame for more than 30 years (John 5).

God's strength is made perfect in our weakness (need). So, tell Him what's wrong! Open your mouth and share your insecurities, fears, hurts, and doubts. Talk to Him as you would with a friend and tell Him whatever is going on inside of you.

2 Corinthians 12:9 Amplified Bible (AMP)
But He has said to me, "My grace is sufficient for you [My loving kindness and My mercy are more than enough—always available—regardless of the situation]; for [My] power is being perfected [and is completed and shows itself most effectively] in [your] weakness." Therefore, I will all the more gladly boast in my weaknesses, so that the power of Christ [may completely enfold me and] may dwell in me.

Choose to give Him all of you. The Bibles says to cast your cares on Him because He cares for you.

1 Peter 5:7 Amplified Bible (AMP)
Casting all your cares [all your anxieties, all your worries, and all your concerns, once and for all] on Him, for He cares about you [with deepest affection, and watches over you very carefully].

Isn't that wonderful? God cares! He doesn't want you to be weighed down by the issues of life, but God can't fix anything you won't give to Him. Many times, we only want to show God our strengths, by holding on and keeping everything to ourselves.

We are trained to deal with ourselves and people in a safe way, showing only our good sides. Through social media, dating, and working, we only like to expose our best versions. We crop, filter, and edit ourselves and leave only what looks good. We only broadcast our finished projects. We fear the rejection of not adding up or not being enough. So, we put on masks to cover our real selves in front of others. We dress up in hopes that they don't see how damaged and broken we really are.

This not only prevents us from entering deep into vulnerable relationships, but it starts to distort our self-image.

When we wear masks for long periods of time we become out of touch with reality and with what is really going on in our lives. And if we are not careful, we could end up losing ourselves in the process. Eventually there will be hard consequences to face from living that way.

We were designed to live from the inside out and not the outside in. When you live from the outside in, eventually your life will fall apart because there is nothing "real" holding it together. Just like trying to build a house on a weak foundation, it just won't be tolerated for too long. Be careful not to build a world for yourself to live in as an escape from God and the reality of your life.

When it comes to developing our relationships with God, we don't need to be fearful or guarded because He has already accepted us and is committed to love us unconditionally. To live a successful life as a believer, this is something we must get deep down into our hearts. We must wholeheartedly believe this to be true and live life from this truth.

Too often, we forget that God created us, and therefore He already knows our pains and sufferings. He is all too familiar with our shortcomings and understands everything that we are going through.

Some of you reading this avoid spending time with God or only show Him your strength because you feel inadequate. For others, the gap in your relationship maybe due to deeply rooted hurts you haven't dealt with. Others may fear that God has changed his mind about them because of something they did or said. It could be the pain of losing a loved one, an unfair situation you faced, bad divorce, or unexpected layoff that has kept you from fully opening your heart to God.

Whatever the case may be, God knows! He knows everything about you. The bible says He even knows the number of hairs on your head (Luke 12:7). God knows you and He loves you more than you could ever imagine. There is nothing you could ever do to change that. Isn't that amazing? There is nothing you could ever do to separate yourself from His love (Romans 8:31-39).

Some of you might be wondering as you read this, if God knows me so well, why do I have to tell Him anything? God desires to have a *real* relationship with you. Just like you have relationships with your friends and family. You spend time with them, you talk with them, you share stories with them. God desires the same. Just think about it, God sent His Son to die so that He could enter into a relationship with you! That is how valuable you are to Him. God has a special purpose for your life and He paid the ultimate price for you! God loves you and longs to be with you and love on you, so let Him.

John 3:16 New International Version (NIV)
For God so loved the world that he gave his one and only Son, that whoever believes in him shall not perish but have eternal life.

Someone Is Waiting On You

A few years ago, I went to a Christian Conference in Texas and a well-known international minister was speaking. She began to tell a story that I will never forget. She explained how God had been using her to deliver and rescue victims of human sex trafficking in various nations worldwide. On one of her missions, she was speaking to a group of women that were staying in a recovery center. While ministering to the women about the love of Christ and the benefits of knowing and having a personal relationship with Him, another woman overheard her from another room and started screaming and yelling "If God is real and He loves us so much and if all of this that you're telling us is true, what took you so long to rescue us? Why would God allow us to suffer for so long?"

The minister paused and told the woman, "I don't know what I was doing in my life that was so important that it got in the way of me pursuing my purpose earlier in life, but I do know that I'm here now and I'm committed to helping you in whatever way that I can."

This story always reminds me that someone needs what I have. And someone needs what you have too. You are the answer to somebody's prayer. There is someone waiting on you to get bold for God and move in the direction of your purpose.

It's urgent that you pursue Christ and what He is calling you to do. God has hidden treasure in you and the world is waiting for it to manifest.

Romans 8:19 New International Version (NIV)
For the creation waits in eager expectation for the children of God to be revealed.

You may not see all the pieces of God's plan yet, but He will reveal them to you, step by step, as you open your heart and let Him in. But again, it all starts with trusting Him, receiving His love and believing in His Word. Place yourself in the hands of the craftsman and let Him make your life a work of art.

Philippians 1:6 Amplified Bible (AMP)
6 I am convinced and confident of this very thing, that He who has begun a good work in you will [continue to] perfect and complete it until the day of Christ Jesus [the time of His return].

Philippians 1:6 is a great scripture because it confirms that God is *doing* the work. When the circumstances of life are overwhelming, and you feel like things are not going your way, you can rest knowing that He is going to finish what He started in you. Amen? That gets me excited!

Many people start, but very rarely do they finish. For example, many people get married, but can they stay married? Many people start working out, but do they commit themselves to the process long enough to see results and lose weight?

Finishing or getting to the end of something requires a different level of force, endurance, and fortitude than what is required to begin.

I am so happy that God is not like people. Everything God starts, He finishes. God even knows the end of a thing before the beginning, so whatever you see started in your life, if you continue to walk with God you can be sure to see the end of it. He will not leave you in the pain of the in-between. But, you need to be willing to stick with the process. You must have a made-up mind to cross the finish line with God.

This scripture is encouraging because it communicates that God is committed to your finish, no matter what! You are not in this alone. On your worst day, when you feel like giving up, God is still committed to your finish. When it feels like the giants in your life are too big to defeat. In those tough situations when you think to yourself, "I have struggled with this for way too long, I will never be able to change..." Just remember, you don't have to make it all happen on your own.

Isn't that good news?

God is committed to your success. As you acknowledge Him in all that you do, He will direct your path and finish the good work He started in you.

Jeremiah 29:11 New International Version (NIV)
For I know the plans I have for you," declares the Lord, "plans to prosper you and not to harm you, plans to give you hope and a future.

God *knows* the plans that He has for you. You didn't buy this book or pick it up by accident, there is a purpose for you reading it. When we walk with God, He gives purpose to everything. He is intentional and knows how to get your attention. I believe that as you continue to seek God with your full heart, that He will begin to reveal Himself to you in a new way or even show Himself to you for the very first time.

I thought it would be a good idea to secure our gains from this chapter by you conditioning your heart to receive what God has for you during your break free journey. Say this prayer with me:

I thank you Lord, that you who have begun a good work in me, is faithful to complete it in the name of Jesus! I believe that as I draw near to you, you will draw nearer to me. Thank you Lord for revealing your truth and love to me and for showing me who I am in Christ. Lord I repent for any and every way that I have knowingly or unknowingly sabotaged the work that you're doing in me. Lord, help me to walk in agreement with you and not against you concerning the plans you have for my life. Help me to see myself the way you see me, through the cross, through the finished work of Jesus. I count all past sources of my confidence as worthless and put my hope and expectation in you. I discover daily your plan for my life and move forward in excellence toward my destiny. I open my heart to you and cast my cares upon you because you care for me. Your word says that the battle is not mine and that you always cause me to triumph in Christ Jesus! Lord, I thank you in advance for the victory of being whole, set free, and becoming the best version of myself in Jesus's name. Amen!

Listed are some verses to help you reinforce what we went over in this chapter. Read them out loud. Pray them over yourself, post them on your mirror; do whatever you need to do to remind yourself that it's "all good."

Philippians 1:6
James 4:8
John 16:13
2 Corinthians 10:12
Psalm 139:14
Psalm 62:5
1 Peter 5:7
2 Corinthians 2:14

CHAPTER 2

LOCATE YOURSELF

I'm going to ask you to be really, *really* honest with yourself. No one will know the answer to these questions but you and God. Take a moment right now to ask yourself, "Am I living my life by who God says I am or by who I say I am? Am I experiencing God's best for my life?"

I'm sure there are desires in your heart, but are those desires *actually* manifesting? Are those desires manifesting in the way and at the *level* you would like them to? If not, are you in the process of doing the work to make them manifest?

For example, you might have a strong desire to be married, but are you positioning yourself and taking time out of your busy life to meet new people? Maybe you are trying to lose weight, but are you consistently working out and eating the right foods for weight loss to occur? Here's the truth, **everyone wants the promise, but nobody wants the process!** I'm sure you've heard this before; can you walk your talk? Or as I like to say it, are you walking or just talking? Meaning, are you taking action? Doing something? Making a difference in your *own* life?

Before you can get a breakthrough in an area of your life, you must first identify where you are. It's just like being at a mall that you are unfamiliar with trying to find the Sephora (my favorite) or whatever store you like best. When you look at the store locator (i.e., map) there is usually a star or some sort of symbol that says, "You are here". Once you see that symbol you know how far away you are from your destination and you can decide the best route to take to get there. Life is the same way. Once you get into the TRUTH about who you are and where you are, you can see the different paths available to you and act towards getting to your destination. As Christians, we have a helper, the Holy Spirit, that guides us into all truth and reveals to us the best path to take (John 16:13). How awesome it that? However, if we are in denial about who we are and where we are, we can't even get there! I believe this is one of the major blessing blockers of many believers - self-deception.

Understanding yourself and getting into the truth about where you are and who you are can be tough, but it is the key to getting results in your life. So, think about all the different areas of your life and ask yourself, is there a difference between who I think I am and who I'm being? Are my beliefs and actions congruent? Bottom line...if you're not getting results...you must ignite your courage and consider your ways.

Haggai 1:5-7 New International Version (NIV)
5 Now this is what the Lord Almighty says: "Give careful thought to your ways. 6 You have planted much, but harvested little. You eat, but never have enough. You drink, but never have your fill. You put on clothes, but are not warm. You earn wages, only to put them in a purse with holes in it. 7 This is what the Lord Almighty says: "Give careful thought to your ways.

Discover Your Why

If you are not getting results in your life or you answered no to any of the questions asked at the beginning of the chapter, ask yourself "Why?" "Why am I *not* getting results?" "What's blocking or stopping me?"

You need to get to the root of your "Why" before you ever start working on it. Otherwise you could spend your entire life in denial about who you are being and never truly experience God's best for your life. Even worse, you can waste your life trying to change symptoms without ever understanding the sickness.

Unfortunately, many people do this. They continue down the path of life, without ever checking in with themselves. They get so wrapped up in creating and maintaining an image, with make-up, hair, clothes, work, money, status, social media, relationships, or whatever it is; that they totally neglect their reality. I decree and declare in the name of Jesus - this will not be you!

Luke 21:34 New International Version (NIV)
"Be careful, or your hearts will be weighed down with carousing, drunkenness and the anxieties of life, and that day will close on you suddenly like a trap.

The issues and worries of life can derail us from receiving God's best. That is why we need to guard our hearts with diligence and be vigilant about what we allow inside.

I don't know what your exact "Why" is because I don't know your story. However, many people accumulate behaviors and attributes that are not authentic to their "real selves" because of positive or negative experiences they have faced in the past. Some people call these coping mechanisms. For example, someone may feel the need to buy gifts for people all the time because they want to win friends. Giving is not wrong, but if there is a hidden motive behind the giving, then; *Houston we have a problem!*

The root of that person's giving could be that they are afraid of rejection and *because* they have been rejected in the past they want to make sure it doesn't happen again! More importantly, they want to be loved and accepted by others. So, on the surface, they see themselves as a giver and they want others to see them as a giver as well, but really, they are manipulating situations to subconsciously get what they want by gift giving.

Can you see the difference between the image they've created for themselves and the facts about who they are *actually* being? Were you able to locate their "why"? The image they've created and are working hard to uphold is "I'm a giver" but the fact is that they are subconsciously or consciously manipulating people to win friends and/or to get reactions from others that will validate and reinforce their worth. The person's "why" is fear of rejection.

Not understanding multiple "Why's" in your life could become a barrier to your destiny and ultimately sabotage the relationships God brings into your life. I like to call these barriers "destiny detours" - undetected negative patterns that keep you from becoming your best self and living the life you are God-destined to live.

You cannot become all God has called you to be until you identify these patterns. They will continue to show their ugly face again and again until you crack the code. At first you may not notice them, they may even seem normal to you but if you are following God and have ears to hear (Mark 4:9), the Holy Spirit will eventually point them out (hopefully you'll listen).

I believe this is one of the ways Satan gets into people's lives and robs them of their true hearts desires. **Whatever you cannot detect or define, you definitely cannot defeat.** Discover the "Why's" behind the behavioral patterns in your life so you can get off the *destiny detour* and back onto the streets of success.

I remember one time when I was dating a guy several years ago. We were out on one of our first dates, eating sushi at a restaurant in my home town. We were having a great time and I was enjoying. We were cracking jokes, laughing together, I was being sweet, funny, and flirtatious. You know, all that good stuff people do on dates.

Suddenly, I received a phone call and someone told me something. I became extremely disappointed. I basically got bad news. Right then and there, I got so angry! I ended up flipping out on the person that was on the other end of the phone. After I finished, I simply hung up the phone and went right back to the date, as if nothing had happened.

But the guy I was on a date with, looked and me and said; "Ashley, you are so sweet, so kind, so nice. I was just wondering why you responded like that to whoever was on the phone". I remember it so clearly, he said, "That reaction does not fit who you are."

I was clueless. I literally sat there staring at him with this perplexed face like, "What are you talking about?" I had been acting like that all my life and nobody had ever called me out on it. I wasn't even sure why I acted like that in the first place. I had no good answer for this guy. After taking in his observation of my response, I was embarrassed. One, because of my actual response; but two because I honestly didn't know that what I was doing was wrong. I was a new Christian and I had no idea about forgiveness and loving people that hurt me.

All of this led me to do some self-reflecting. When I got home, after he dropped me off, I started to ask God questions. I spent time in His presence, trying to figure out why I would snap at people like this. Through prayer and journaling, I would ask God, "Why am I like this? Why do I talk to people in such a harsh way when I feel disappointed?"

Then the Lord began to reveal to me how I had been treated poorly by people I loved, when I made mistakes or when I missed the mark. And because people that I loved had been harsh with me, I got used to this kind of behavior and somehow began to replicate it in my own life and relationships.

It wasn't until that moment that I realized that it was a problem and that I had a decision to make. Did I want to be like that or not?

I remember talking to the Lord and crying about it. All the while hoping I hadn't ruined my chances with the guy.

And although what God was doing inside of me was never about this guy liking me in the first place, but about me becoming more Christ like, I was happy to learn that the guy still liked me after this incident.

After this situation, I made a decision. I didn't want this to be a part of who I was anymore. And from that day forward, I started to work on it. It didn't go away right away. I had to work on it, repeatedly. Even as my walk with God continued, this was one of those things that was always trying to rise and choke the fruitfulness of my life, work, and relationships.

I had to really learn how to manage this. So, I began to fight the habit I had with God's word. I found all the scriptures I could on love and the power of words and I started meditating on them like a crazy person! I made flash cards and post it notes and put them in the house and inside my car. I would say them out loud and read them repeatedly. I continued to be diligent in my process of changing. The two scriptures that I remember rehearsing the most were, "I am rooted and grounded in love," and "I am increasing and abounding in love for others" (Ephesians 3:17, 1 Thessalonians 3:12).

I stood on these scriptures, verses that I still confess over my life to this day; until they became so rooted into my heart, that they started to transform me from the inside out.

I realized that this was not something that God had put in me. This was simply a learned behavior. But God promised that

He would uproot anything that He didn't plant. I took that at heart and walked everyday believing in that promise. Occasionally, the enemy tries to take be back into my old self and old patterns, but I am quick to remind him that I have already overcome because of the love of Jesus!

In this specific situation, I didn't know what was behind my reaction. Your girl didn't know that she could go from zero to 100, real quick. It wasn't until the Holy Spirit confronted me about his behavior that I was able to fully understand it and then change.

I discovered the "why" behind my behavior and everything in between. Understanding this helped me pin point where the devil was trying to sabotage my spiritual growth and success. God used that date to illuminate an area of my heart that he wanted to touch and ever since that day He has continued to mature me and show me how to love.

I encourage you to search for the behavioral patterns in your life that need to be changed. Discover the "why" behind them, because your life depends on it. Go to God in prayer and allow him to uproot anything that would hinder you from living an abundant life. I know this is not an easy thing to do, but God is with you and you can do all things through Christ Jesus who strengthen you. Be strong and courageous!

Discover The Truth

As you discover who you are and who you have been lately, it's most important to understand who God says you are. Whatever He says about you is crucial for you and your life as a believer. There are facts and then there is the *truth*, God's truth.

If you have ever watched a movie with a trial scene, you have probably heard this before "Do you swear to tell the truth, the whole truth, and nothing but the truth, so help you God? Have you ever wondered why they make people say this as they hold their hand on the Bible?

I believe it is because placing your hand on top of a Bible transforms the truth from being relative to being absolute, simply because the Bible carries weight, leaving no room for lying, cheating, or deceiving. If the witness is later found to have lied, they can be charged with the crime of perjury. The Bible sworn testimony is there to remind people of the core values written in the Word of God, values that have truth as their banner.

God's Word is the truth, *your* truth. It is the highest form of reality for your life. But you must choose to believe in it, for it to transform you. So, the question is, do you really *believe* that what God says about you in His word is true for you?

Sometimes, it is easier for us to believe it to be true for those we love and the people around us, than for ourselves. But you must believe, deep in your own heart, that His word is true for you and your life. This is important to understand because whatever you believe you will ultimately become. The Word of God will be powerless in your life, if you don't believe it to be true *for you.*

Sometimes we can even believe God for ourselves in some areas in our life, but have difficulty doing so in other areas. This kind of "selective faith" come from two places. First, from what you believe to be true about God. Second, from what you believe to be true about yourself.

For example, maybe you are struggling to have a baby and you know another family that is struggling, too. It may be easier for you to believe that God will give the family a child, but you may struggle to believe it for yourself. This basically happens because you subconsciously believe that God loves them enough to do this for the family, but somehow you don't all the way believe that He can do it for you.

The same could be true for finances. Maybe you feel like God could give financial success to someone else, but not you. Or that God will give everyone else a nice marriage, but you will stay single forever. Maybe you believe the best for people's career opportunities, but feel forgotten by God in that area.

The truth is that God can do anything for anybody at any time, not because of your performance, but based on His unfailing love. A love that makes no difference, a love that surrendered the life if His son, not for the ones who had it figured out, but for all humankind.

The bottom line is you may not feel worthy enough to receive God's favor, you may think you have made too many mistakes, you may even think God doesn't love you as much as He loves someone else. But He does love you and you are worthy of His favor and affection. Not because of anything you have done but because of what Jesus did on the cross.

The problem with this kind of thinking, is that it affects your faith and without faith it is impossible to please God (Hebrews 11:6). Everything we receive from God comes by faith (Romans 4:16). So, don't take this lightly because whatever you believe about God will ultimately determine what you experience through Him.

1 Thessalonians 2:13 New International Version (NIV)
And we also thank God continually because, when you received the word of God, which you heard from us, you accepted it not as a human word, but as it actually is, the word of God, which is indeed at work in you who believe.

Let me give you an example of what I'm talking about. I have a friend. She is naturally outgoing and fun, but for some reason in front of other people she would turn into a completely different person. Do you know anyone like that? She would almost become non- verbal in front of others, not saying more than a couple of words. She would even make weird gestures and do things I'd never seen her do before when we were together alone. It always left me confused! I would be thinking in my mind "What are you doing? or "Why are you acting so weird?".

She did this so many times throughout our friendship. Finally, one day I got the courage to ask her about the behavior and she began to open up and tell me that she *believed* that people did not like her and felt like they would brush her off and be rude. As a result, she would try her best to become invisible in front of others. I asked her if any of the people we knew had ever mistreated her that way and she replied no. After talking for quite a while, we were able to "crack the code" on her belief system. There were incidents in her childhood with groups of people where her opinion was either laughed at or not valued.

Because of those experiences, she developed a fear of being rejected and as a result, she would turn into this created version of herself - the opposite of who she truly was - to protect herself from potentially being rejected and being hurt. This "created version" of her was a habit. She had been acting like this for years before our code cracking conversation. Her belief system was turning her into someone she wasn't and deep down it was making her feel depressed. She attended church and she knew God's word, but she never *believed* God's word and made it true for her *own* life. By default, her beliefs about herself were shaped by the opinions, conversations, and thoughts of people from her past, instead of the word of God. In the Bible, it says that we are accepted in the beloved. That is her *truth*. The highest reality for her life. Regardless of what she believes or what she experienced. She is accepted, loved and care for and so are you!

Choose to Believe

Once you discover the truth about who God says you are in His word, you must decide to believe it. If you don't make this decision, you will go back and forth for the rest of your life about who you really are. God does not do this for you. Believing is a decision. Once you have a made-up mind that you are going to believe what God says about you and your life, you can start moving forward and go somewhere. Believing is the first step to getting the shot at seeing the promises of God fulfilled in your life.

Some of you reading might be wondering; how do I know if I believe? Or how do I start believing? The Bible says that it is with your heart that you believe and are justified, and it is with your mouth that you confess and are saved (Romans 10:9-10). Believing is an act of faith, it comes out of our hearts. Our heart is the production center of our life. Whatever images get into our heart; God has designed us to produce. The Bible tells us to guard our hearts for this very reason.

Proverbs 4:23 New International Version (NIV)
Above all else, guard your heart, for everything you do flows from it.

So, if we know the issues of life come from our hearts, whatever we see happening in our lives reflects that. For example, if you always find yourself running out of money, chances are the shortage is not in your pocket, it is coming from your heart.

The Bible says that as a man thinks in his heart, so is he (Proverbs 23:7). When I first read this I thought to myself, -wow we can think in our hearts, not just in our minds?

Yes, we can!

And as we do, we become those things. A man thinks; therefore, he is. To think in your heart means to learn to discern God's truth and to rely on His wisdom.

This is less about trusting our first mind and more about learning to discern what is in our hearts and what is from God versus what comes from ourselves, the enemy, or other sources. We need to examine our hearts and ensure it aligns with God's will. Once we discover what is living on the inside of us, then we can make a choice about what we believe.

We have to self-check and also allow the Holy Spirit to reveal beliefs that are blocking the seeds of truth being planted in us through God's word. So that our seeds have the opportunity to be nourished appropriately and endure their process of eventually becoming fruit. Fruit that remains and can be perceived as edible by others.

John 15:8 New International Version (NIV)
8 This is to my Father's glory, that you bear much fruit, showing yourselves to be my disciples.

God has a lot of things that He wants to do in you and through you. But before that can happen you must settle in your heart once and for all that you believe God, His word and that everything He has said is true for you and your life. Once you make that quality decision and begin to take actions that align with that truth, your life will never be the same.

Self-Check

Many people know the word of God and many people confess the word over their lives, but they are not seeing results. Instead of self-checking they end up blaming God or people around them. When we are doing the same thing over and over and it's not producing a result, we need to do some self-checking.

Are you in action? Have you stepped out in faith? Are you being *both* a hearer and a doer of the Word? God does not change and as I already mentioned, He is no respecter of people. He doesn't pick and choose who to help. God wants to help us all. God does not show favoritism. (Acts 10:34)

So, if your *neighbor* can get a spouse...so can you! If your *cousin* can start a business, so can you! It's easier to blame others rather than looking at ourselves, but there is no power in that. The only person that can stop you from living the good life God planned for you is YOU! It sounds cliché, but it's true. You can blame the pastor, your mama, ex-boyfriend, whoever, but it will not move you forward in life. It takes courage to look at yourself, to see if you are playing the blame game and then take new actions toward being responsible and accountable for your own life.

It is important to be truthful with ourselves because the enemy loves deception. Many people are walking around deceived because they haven't slowed down and taken the time to look inside themselves and ask the tough questions. For example, if you've experienced a breakup, don't just go on to the next relationship without looking at why the relationship with your "Boo" or "Bae" didn't work out. Take a moment and ask the Holy Spirit to show you your role in the demise.

You cannot be a victim and be victorious at the same time. You must decide. A victim's mentality says I can't do it because they don't like me. I can't change because this is who I am, I've always been like this. A victorious mindset says, "I always win!" (2 Corinthians 2:14), "I can do all things through Christ Jesus who strengthens me" (Philippians 4:13) and "All things are working for my good!" (Romans 8:28).

A victim mentality blames others regardless of the situation. A victorious mindset takes ownership.

Remember, there are two sides to every story. So, if you have any broken relationships in your life, examine yourself, take ownership of the part you played in it, but most importantly learn from your mistakes.

Many times, we are on autopilot, just thinking and doing whatever we believe is right and then we look up and wonder why our situation or life doesn't reflect the vision we wanted to achieve or the dreams we had treasured in our hearts.

When this happens, it's simply because we didn't take enough time to self- check. As people of God, we must be committed to living the truth long enough to see results.

Self - checking and embracing the truth is like when Jesus said to Simon and Andrew in Matthew 4:18-20 *"follow me and I will make you fishers of men."* Before Jesus showed up, Simon and Andrew were fine catching fish. Being fishermen is what they identified with, but when Jesus said follow me and I will make you fishers *of* men, he was introducing them to the truth about who they really were, on the next level, the upgraded versions of themselves. Simon and Andrew had to decide. They could either stay with what was familiar or they could believe the truth and become who Jesus called them to be. Simon and Andrew had to do a self-check. Jesus knew they were fine catching fish, but He also knew that if they followed Him (the truth) they would do exceedingly and abundantly better.

Challenge yourself to start taking time out to self-check and reflect on your decisions and the condition of your life consistently. Spend quality time with God daily and begin to ask yourself those tough questions. Get into the truth of God's word and get to know yourself better. Most importantly, get to know God better! He has an amazing plan for your future and I *know* you want to discover it. God is near you, He listens to your prayers. Just talk to Him honestly and openly. He will answer.

Psalm 145:18 New International Version (NIV)
The Lord is near to all who call on him, to all who call on him in truth.

CHAPTER 3

HEARERS & DOERS

A large amount of people end up being commentators and spectators instead of being participators in the world and in their own life. I don't believe this happens on purpose. I mean, nobody wakes up and says, "You know what, I am going to *do* nothing with my life". Of course not. We want our lives to be significant, to have meaning and purpose. But, people who tend to lean more on the side of being commentators and spectators have subconsciously become that way over time. I am suggesting that they did not start out that way. Usually, if you search into their history, there is something painful they have experienced, a crisis, trauma, something that has subconsciously paralyzed their ambition, or desire for more and over time they become less intentional and enthusiastic about "doing" anything extraordinary with their life. I believe that this sneaks up on people like a lion on a gazelle out in the wild. Their distracted attitude is barely noticeable until one day they look up and realize that this is not what they wanted their life to look like. Maybe what I am saying here does not apply to you, but if it does know that God is able to deliver you from living this way. He is willing and ready to help you take your life back. Not just one part of it, but all of it. But to do so, you must be willing to "Hear" and then "Do" whatever and I do mean whatever God says.

"Hearing" and "doing" the word of God is not the same. Sometimes we can hear and talk about something so much, that it feels like we are actually doing it - even when we are not. Being both a hearer and a doer is another major key to breaking free in your life. Being one and not the other simply won't do.

It's like cooking food and eating it. Let's say you went to the store and bought some ingredients. You got back home and cooked a nice meal. But until you eat it, it will do you no good.

The same is for our spiritual life. You can go to church, read your Bible, get yourself some good quotes and amazing verses, and truth that has the potential to feed your soul and transform your heart. But, it won't do you any good until you actually get it inside of you and let it nurture you from the inside out.

The problem is that most people understand this principle intellectually on some level, but they are often challenged when it comes to applying it to their lives.

Knowing that exercise is good for you won't help you until you start moving. Knowing that you should be responsible with your finances won't help you prosper until you start spending wisely or making a budget. You've got to walk the talk if you want to get somewhere. But you've got to walk with God if you want to get to somewhere purposeful.

It is only when you obey God's voice and are acting on what the word of God says, that you are truly living by faith. And when you do this, you are communicating to God that you are both a hearer and a doer.

James 1:22 Amplified Bible (AMP)
22 But prove yourselves doers of the word [actively and continually obeying God's precepts], and not merely listeners [who hear the word but fail to internalize its meaning], deluding yourselves [by unsound reasoning contrary to the truth].

90% of people spend their time hearing and learning about things they will never actually do. Many love to hear the word of God, read books, and listen to other messages that tell them how to live their best lives, but often, struggle when it comes to applying what they've learned to their lives. I come across so many people who attend church *all* the time, they love their pastor and can quote every catchy phrase, but they are not actually *living* the word of God.

We must be careful not to become hung up on motivational messages and sermons. Attending weekly church on Wednesdays and Sundays, keenly listening for the next rhema word, and walking around with anointing oil in our pocket, but *never truly* allowing the Word of God to get all up in our business, and penetrate our hearts.

Do you know what I mean? We need to be the real deal. In the famous words of Rocky Balboa, from the movie Rocky VI, life is not always sunshine and rainbows. We all come up on hard times and we are all works in progress, and will continue to be as long as we live. But, if we are believers, our lives should mirror the scriptures and we should be able to see some results, or at least the *progression* of the promises of God being fulfilled in our lives.

In James 1, verses 23 to 25, we read a very interesting metaphor of the difference between hearers and doers of the Word of God.

James 1:23-25 New International Version (NIV)
Anyone who listens to the word but does not do what it says is like someone who looks at his face in a mirror and, after looking at himself, goes away and immediately forgets what he looks like. But whoever looks intently into the perfect law that gives freedom, and continues in it—not forgetting what they have heard, but doing it— they will be blessed in what they do.

Is the Word of God the anchor in your daily decision making? Do you apply what you read? What would happen if God Himself came and tested the quality of your willingness to act on His word, whatever He has placed in your heart to accomplish? Buying that building? Taking that mission trip? Starting that business? Would you pass the test? When Christ is in us, our lives should be a testament of that reality.

2 Corinthians 13:5 New International Version (NIV)
5 Examine yourselves to see whether you are in the faith; test yourselves. Do you not realize that Christ Jesus is in you—unless, of course, you fail the test?

As believers, we must examine ourselves. The Bible is our mirror. Through this examination, we can determine for ourselves whether or not we are in faith, if we truly believe, and if the promises of God are manifesting in our lives.

We do ourselves a disservice when we create fantasies to live in that separate us from the truth of the reality we are living in day to day. Our life will only begin to drastically change when we have the courage to tell ourselves the truth (good, bad, and ugly) and take action. It is when we begin to *consistently* step out on faith that our lives drastically change, and for the better.

Ears to Hear

To be doers of the Word, we must humble ourselves under the mighty hand of God and position ourselves to hear Him. Sometimes, we get so caught up with what we want and how we want it, that it prevents us from hearing the voice of God. It is so important that we hear God's voice, because His voice is the only carrier of truth. Without the truth, we are walking around in darkness. And how much can you find or figure out if it's dark?

We must be careful to make sure that our voice, or the voices around us, do not overpower or override God's whisper in our life. When God speaks to us He doesn't always tell us what we want to hear, and that is why at times we can become tempted to tune Him out. As a result, we can end up being led astray by our own interests, ideas, emotions, and opinions. Although God loves us, He is not interested in negotiating with us when it comes to obeying His voice. When coming into the kingdom of God, you lose your right to always be "right". Whatever God says, is the final word. His voice must become the final authority in your life. That is the only way you can be sure to unlock your full potential and insure your life's success.

In developing our relationship with God and learning to hear His voice, there are some challenges that could become barriers to hearing Him. We need to be careful not to let our friendship with God override our honor and respect for Him.

Let me explain further. Sometimes, people can get so comfortable with God, in a nonchalant way that they minimize what He says to them. Their own thoughts and opinions end up carrying more weight than His Word and voice. I believe that this is a result of people thinking and treating God like He is a person.

God is not a person. He is the great I Am, the almighty, the creator of the universe. He is the beginning and the end, the alpha and the omega. He is our father, our provider, our maker, our refuge, our savior, and our strength. And yes, our friend! Do you see where I am going with this? God is our friend, He is understanding, loving, and supportive, but He is so much more than that. We need to keep a full understanding of who He is, so we can live confident, but humble. Feeling safe under His wing, without losing our reverence for Him.

Without careful attention to our walk with God, we can end up transferring our habits and behaviors with people into our relationship with Him.

For example, I have seen this happen when people neglect to respect the gifts and the god in their colleagues, friends, or spouses. When this happens, it prevents them from being able to receive whatever God might be trying to get to them through that person. This can become problematic.

For example, there are times I've seen people get too comfortable with my Pastor. They hear him so much, that they take him and his messages for granted. As a result, they miss out on the many benefits of implementing what he says. I can also remember a time that one of my business mentors told me that she made all her clients address her by using her official title, Dr., because she felt like people took her less seriously when she allowed them to address her simply by her first name. Not only that, but she expressed that when she allowed them to call her by her first name alone, that they saw her as more of a girlfriend instead of an expert in her field or trusted advisor. When this happened, it would directly affect her ability to deliver certain concepts and information to those individuals. On the flip side, it would affect their ability to receive from her.

It is important to remember that God desires us to experience Him as a friend, but not to the point of discrediting the respect or reverence that we should have for Him. When you keep your honor for God high, you can more easily assess His voice.

When you are disobedient to God's voice because His Word does not carry enough weight in your life and in your daily decisions, over time, you subconsciously train your spirit to ignore Him. If this continues in the long-run, you could potentially deceive yourself and think you are hearing from God, but, you're simply listening to yourself. Either way, it is still problematic.

The main thing God wants when He asks for our obedience is to bless us. The reality is that He knows better than anybody else, the blessings that will come if we simply walk by faith and follow His lead.

I remember when I got engaged to my boyfriend at the time and I thought we were meant to be together. I mean, on paper it all looked perfect. He was a pastor's kid, grew up in the church, he did ministry, and was a very accomplished athlete. Come on, it felt like I hit the jackpot.

But there were also many red flags. Mostly, he was dishonest, and I could feel it in my spirit. I didn't ignore the red flags, but when I brought them up, he was very crafty at reassuring me that everything was okay when in reality, things were not.

Also, seeing him serve at church every Sunday didn't help. I mean, he played the part so well, and knew how to say all the right things. But at least at that point in his life, there was a disconnect between what he allowed people to see and who he really was.

After a lot of struggle and prayer, just 30 days before my wedding, I called it off. And let me just say, this was one of the toughest decisions I have ever made. I loved him and had invested so much into the relationship so even after calling off the wedding, I decided to stay in and work on the relationship. The problem is that where God was giving me a way out, I saw a chance to arrange things and began to invest all of my energy into fixing this relationship. We went to counseling, we talked about the things that needed to change. I was working so hard to make things "right" but everything was still wrong. After prayer and much reflection, I eventually realized that I was so focused on my desire of getting married that I was completely misinterpreting God's intentions for me.

We Must Be Careful Not to Let Our Motives Manipulate God's Voice.

Eventually I mustered up the courage and broke up with him, and things in my life started to get back in order, until he pursued me again. And then can you believe it? I gave him another chance.

But regardless of my effort, that was not what God wanted for me. The problem is that in situations like this, there are so many things that can damage the way we relate to God's voice. One thing that gets in the way is holding on to our own desires above God's will. Another would be the voices of other people, who might mean well, but only end up confusing us more. A big one is our concern with people's approval. In order to obey God's voice, I had to forget about people's opinions, let go of my own desires and focus solely on trusting Him.

But this is the amazing thing about God. When I finally decided to trust and obey Him, he immediately confirmed that I was on the right track and affirmed His love for me.

This is how He did it. I was visiting a church shortly after all the drama with my boyfriend unfolded and a minister called me up to the front of the church and prophesied to me. The word she gave me expressed that God allowed the heartbreak I had experienced from that relationship and that He allowed it to fall apart because He wanted to take my life in a different direction. God expressed through this minister that there were somethings I needed to experience on my own before God could move me forward and so that I could encounter the next dimension of my purpose. As she spoke these words over me, I knew in my heart they were from God.

I remember thinking, "Wow!"

The possibility of stunting my growth and further delaying my destiny was one that really made me reflect. I knew deep down in my heart that staying in a relationship would never be worth missing God's plans and purposes for my life. But if any of you reading this have ever been in a similar situation, you know that obeying God in times like these can be easier said than done.

Looking back, I am so glad that I listened to God's voice. I have been blessed in countless ways because of my willingness to both "hear" and "do" what God told me. Since then, so much has happened that I need to write another book! And maybe I will, but for now, let's just take it one book at a time.

Anyway, lot of times we might think that we are not seeing the promises of God fulfilled in our lives because God is taking too long, but the truth is that many times, we are the ones delaying our breakthroughs.

Anytime you feel like God is sending you off, spend more time in His presence and in His Word, because usually, this feeling comes from a miscommunication between us and God. Reading the Bible and spending time with God will always help you begin to hear Him more accurately.

All in all, we must be willing to let go of our motives and agenda to hear God clearly. When what *you* want is so loud, it will end up blocking God's voice completely.

Look, God is not interested in fighting with you in order to bless you. He is patient and kind and He will definitely wait for you, but He is not going to force you to listen to His voice. He wants a willing heart that freely obeys and respects Him, not the type of relationship where we obey as an obligation. He will allow you to "Do You" and be led by your own motives and interests as long as you want to. But the consequences for doing so will be great. Be careful not to misuse or abuse the freedom you have been given, as it can derail God's plans and purposes for your life.

I don't know if you've ever heard this before, but God will wait for us to come to the end of ourselves. Meaning, He will wait for you to humble yourself under His authority long enough to listen for his voice. We will always have the choice to receive or to reject Him.

It's like when someone is drowning and battling to stay above water, waving their arms around, and moving frenetically. Their only chance of survival is surrendering. The lifeguard must wait until the person stops fighting with their own strength before attempting to rescue them. If they try to take control while the person is moving their body around all over the place, it could make the situation worse. So, what am I saying?

I believe we are often like that person drowning. We ask for God's help, but then we don't allow Him to takeover. We continue fighting the good fight of faith, still relying on our own strength.

But, it is only when we surrender that we can be saved from whatever we are facing in life. When we choose to slow down and humble ourselves before God, then we can see His mighty hand at work. By this, I don't mean that we don't have a role to play in the process. But first, we must check the posture of our hearts and make sure that our personal agenda is not in competition with God's plans and purposes for our lives.

Just like a little child that subconsciously recognizes his limitations and trusts his parents to supply beyond those limits. We must do what is in our power to do, and then trust God to do the rest.

Matthew 18:3 King James Version (KJV)
3 And said, Verily I say unto you, Except ye be converted, and become as little children, ye shall not enter into the kingdom of heaven.

When children are young, they come to their parents expecting answers and assistance. They ask questions like, when are we leaving? Can I have that? Can you tie my shoe? Children see their parents as the answer and final authority in their life. They depend on their parents to get their needs met. If our perspective is not similar when it comes to God, then we will likely get caught up in moving ahead of Him and doing things our way.

Intentionally or unintentionally, I think we all do this at some point. We get carried away by our own motives and miss God's guidance.

I know there have been many times in my life where I've moved ahead of God, only to turn right back around to meet Him where I originally started in the first place. When this happens, it can be very frustrating. I always end up thinking, why did I walk for so long in the wrong direction? I lost so much time! If I had just followed God, I would be exactly where I need to be.

In fact, I constantly check myself on this a lot, because it is so easy to get caught up in the momentum of life. Sometimes, we can move so fast that we forget to consult God. Over the years though, life has taught me the value of slowing down, seeking Him first and making the time to listen for His voice. It's a trick of the enemy to get you moving so fast, that you completely miss God. Slowing down to hear the voice of God is so important that even when you are pursuing the will of God, at times, He will allow things to completely collapse when you move without yielding to His voice just as a reminder for you to keep him at the center of your plans next time. And then after you seek Him, He will rebuild it all over again.

The problem with moving ahead of God, is that we end up building lives with our limited human reasoning, strength and wisdom. We develop businesses, relationships, careers, churches, school systems, marriages, whatever it is and leave God out. Many times, it's not that what we built was bad or wrong to begin with, but that it will not be sustainable long term or never reach its optimal potential or place because God was not at the center. God doesn't want to see us in the middle of everything, He wants to see himself! Whenever God does not see himself, in you, the plan, the project, or the process, He will allow it to shut down. He will allow life, business, your marriage, your finances, or whatever it is to get uncomfortable. He will shake things up. That is His way of getting our attention. It is his way of reminding us that our human intellect is limited without our divine connection with Him. It is his way of shifting us back into his will and into his way of doing things - doing business, doing marriage, doing finances, doing church, doing life.

God needs to be in the center of everything so that when the results of what we have been working on turn out great, He can get the glory. As a result, people will be drawn to Him and not me or you. That is the goal! For people to be drawn to His love, His power, His wisdom, His strength, and His Word.

At times, you can think something is right because it's popular or because your parents raised you to think so, but if you don't check in with God, things can get messy. A good decision is not always a God-decision.

One time I had a client that was so caught up in doing church work and ministry, that she was constantly talking about it, but she was forgetting to reflect and recognize her own process with God. She was hiding behind people and her performance. It was easier for her to "do" than to be. We must be careful not to focus on "doing" that we neglect listening to or spending time in the presence of God.

I remember one time, a youth organization wanted me to come work for them. When we met, everything seemed right. In all the years I had worked with youth, no other contract had ever matched my gifts or skills like this one.

I worked with them for a couple of weeks. I was having a great time with the kids, but bumping heads with the organization. Things were become progressively uncomfortable. As a result, I started to ask myself some important questions. Was this really the place for me? Did God send me her or did I come on my own terms? I loved working with youth, what was wrong?

They started to ask me for things that were outside of my contract, and on top of that they asked to extend the number of months I was required to work. I knew I had the capacity to do what they were asking of me, and because there was no other opportunity on the horizon, I agreed, and decided to stay.

But still, something didn't feel quite right. In this whole time, I hadn't even checked in with God. So, eventually I decided to quit, but then they convinced me to stay. Later, they decided not to extend my contract and ended up firing me anyway. I am sure that if I had checked in with God, I would have been able to leave the organization before this series of events even happened. I also would have saved some time and energy.

Working with the youth was a good thing, but that was not the right place for me anymore. God had other plans. If I had left when God told me to leave, things would have ended smoother.

Sometimes We Need to Give Up On What We Can See, To Receive From God What We Can't See.

While in that situation, I realized that God did in fact lead me to that opportunity, but it was for a shorter time like I had envisioned.

Although I understood this, I still questioned it. What was I going to do next? I was unsure of what God had in store for me. I was unclear of His next move and plan. And that was tempting me to stay longer than I was supposed to. But once you hear from God, the only proper response is faith, even if you don't understand.

Do you see where I'm going with this? Can you pin it to your own life?

Would you be willing to leave your loving Christian boyfriend, the man that has been there for you, simply because God said that he is not your husband and is time to move on?

What about that job you do so well? Or that comfortable department in church where you serve so faithfully?

Most people listen to God at the beginning, when they need to know where they are going, but when they get there, a lot of them forget to continue to check in with God, and that is where things get kind of difficult.

Looking back into that situation, I do believe that if I had stayed there longer, I would have missed out on a lot of the plans that God had in store for me. I thank God for redirecting me back to where He wanted me, but at that moment, I was distracted. The season was over, I just needed to get up and walk to where God was taking me. No questions asked, no hesitation, just fully trusting Him.

We walk from faith to faith, not from security blanket to security blanket. You were designed to walk by faith and not by sight but that means you must be willing to walk away from your comfort zone.

Faith To Do

When we act on what we hear God say directly to us or in His word, we are in faith. This communicates to God that we believe, that we can be trusted, and that we are both a hearer and a doer.

At times, it can be really tempting to disguise this process of hearing and obeying God with perfect church attendance. I know in my own life there have been seasons where I have struggled with this. I found myself unplugged from my personal relationship with God, but attending church every Wednesday and Sunday. I was completely tuned into my church community and friends, but unplugged from my personal relationship with Christ. Turning my church more into a social gathering and less into a transformational life-giving experience. Maybe you can relate?

I have had to be extremely intentional about checking in with myself and making the proper adjustments in my life to ensure that my focus stays on God and not people or my performance. And although church going is important, perfect church attendance does not directly equate to life success and a strong relationship with God. What we're *doing* in between what we're *hearing* from Sunday to Sunday will ultimately determine the course of our lives and the levels to which we will thrive and succeed.

If we are not intentional, it can be easy to get caught up in performance, "looking like we are living for God", when in reality we are only living for ourselves or to be seen, recognized and affirmed by others. And If we are not mindful our wants can begin to override God's will.

What You Do Should Be Driven By Your Love For God, Not From A Desire For Someone To Love You.

The Bible says that men look at the outer appearance, but God looks at the heart. Are you worried about being liked or about being a light? Are you concerned about honoring God or about pleasing people?

It's the posture of our heart that allows us to obey God's voice, move in faith, and to *do* whatever it is that He is asking us to do.

As I mentioned before, the Bible says without faith it is impossible to please God (Hebrews 11:6). That means we can't please God without both *hearing* and *doing*.

The same way you don't lose weight by hearing and reading about nutrition and exercise. Oh, how I wish this was true! You can't display faith by just hearing about it. You need to take action. You must have faith to "do."

James 2:14-26 The Message (MSG) Faith in Action
14-17 Dear friends, do you think you'll get anywhere in this if you learn all the right words but never do anything? Does merely talking about faith indicate that a person really has it? For instance, you come upon an old friend dressed in rags and half-starved and say, "Good morning, friend! Be clothed in Christ! Be filled with the Holy Spirit!" and walk off without providing so much as a coat or a cup of soup—where does that get you? Isn't it obvious that God-talk without God-acts is outrageous nonsense?

No Shades of Gray

A simple example to help you understand what I mean by *shades of gray* would be like if you were starting to see someone on a personal level. And although time is going by, you are not committed to each other and the purpose of your relationship has not been defined. This leaves both of you, wondering what kind of relationship this is and what you mean to the other person.

Gray areas are comfortable. I get it. But, when it comes to your spiritual development, it is vital to your faith that you steer clear of gray areas or move though them rather quickly because indecision and uncertainty are enemies to your development and destiny. You're hot or your cold. You believe, or you don't. I know this is tough-love, but God wants us to live boldly. Loving God is a decision we make. With Him, it's all or nothing. He doesn't want us stuck in the middle, on the fence or in any shades of gray. He wants us to live our lives with clarity. When we are living in gray areas, there is no light or boundaries and we are more susceptible to life's problems and pitfalls. The devil is always looking for a point of entry into our lives and I promise you that his favorite color is gray! There are many scriptures that support what I am talking about in this section.

James 1:5-8 King James Version (KJV)
If any of you lack wisdom, let him ask of God, that giveth to all men liberally, and up braideth not; and it shall be given him. But let him ask in faith, nothing wavering. For he that wavereth is like a wave of the sea driven with the wind and tossed. For let not that man think that he shall receive any thing of the Lord. A double minded man is unstable in all his ways.

Matthew 5:37 New King James Version (NKJV)
37 But let your 'Yes' be 'Yes,' and your 'No,' 'No.' For whatever is more than these is from the evil one.

When we choose to love God, we are also choosing to become single minded. Meaning, it's His way or no way. We move from our plan, to His plan. The Bible says that when our eyes are single then our bodies are full of light.

People often ask me how I receive results so quickly in my walk with God. But the thing is they haven't seen the entire process I have gone through to get where I am.

Hear me clearly, God is a God of processes. And although He can achieve things in our life in a lightning bolt speed if He wants to, He does not do *everything* fast.

Noah waited 120 years before the predicted rain arrived (Genesis 6 to 8). Joseph waited 13 years before he got out of the pit and entered the palace (Genesis 41: 46). Abraham waited 25 years for his promised son (Genesis 12 to 17), and even Moses waited 40 years in the desert.

There have been many times in my life where God made me wait. However, when something in my life is not going as I expected, I don't entertain the option that something is wrong with God or His Word. I know that God is either making me wait to protect me from something or that there is something that he wants to uproot or mature on the inside of me. And I understand that it all happens for a greater purpose. Most importantly, I do my very best to gain understanding from what I experience. And when you knock on the door of understanding it closes the door to confusion.

Lack of clarity is a thief. It functions like quicksand, sucking up your time, energy, and resources. The longer you live in gray, the more you will suffer financially and otherwise.

Prosperity Loves Clarity.

The enemy knows this and so he tries to confuse you as a strategy to quench your faith. When shades of gray come to cloud your consciousness or dull your senses, turn on a light! The best way to do that is by reading the Word of God. The Bible says it is "a lamp unto our feet and a light unto our path" (Psalm 119:105). The light from the scriptures will force all forms of darkness to leave your mind and they will illuminate your way of escape. So, what am I saying here? Stay lit!

What Are You *Doing*?

Let's say God spoke to you and told you that you're gifted to be a writer. After you hear from God, what do you do? Do you simply listen and let time pass by, or do you start writing and seek God for more revelation about this?

If God gives us clues and tells us what to do next, but we are unwilling to yield to his voice, how can we expect to see His promises manifested in our lives?

There are so many different external and internal barriers that try to block us from unlocking our God-given potential. However, from my experience of working with a variety of people, both in ministry and in business settings there are two subtle mindsets that are not always so easily detected. One, when we decide to follow our own agendas, subconsciously deceiving ourselves into thinking that what we want is God's best or desire for our lives. The second one is when we focus on chasing material blessings instead of the blessing giver. I know most of us don't do this on purpose. Societal norms, mainstream media messages and religious expectations are always trying to replace and or compete with our personal relationships with God. As a result, without even knowing it, we can find ourselves in situations and circumstances that are delaying and derailing God's plans and purposes for our life.

The behaviors that follow these mindsets can go undetected for years if we are not careful to self-check.

The bible says in Matthew chapter 6 verse 33 *"but seek first his kingdom and his righteousness, and all these things will be given to you as well."*

That is the key. We must seek the Lord first, not second, third, or after anything else, including work, friends, activities, and so on. When you *do* this, everything else you need will be added to you. If you spend your life trying to add to yourself instead of letting God add to you, eventually you will become discouraged and depleted. This leads to burn out! God did not design you to operate independent of Him.

Seeking God is not a passive process, it's active. You should listen for God in your conversations, business deals and friendships. Essentially, all aspects of your life. You should seek God when your bank account is experiencing overflow and when it is in overdraft. You should seek God in sunshine and in rain! That's the behavior of a doer.

If you're not looking for God, you'll miss what He's doing.

God made you for more than a dead end job or a job that you hate. I get it — if you don't work, you don't eat, but any occupation that prevents you from tapping into your full potential and fulfilling your purpose is a waste of time. God may use smaller opportunities as a stepping stone or as a starting place to help you work out your potential, as He prepares you for purpose. But, be careful not to become complacent, settling for less than God's best either because you are too afraid to step out on faith, or because your are unwilling to *do* the work that is necessary to develop yourself further. If you want to live a life you love, you have to build one. So, what are you going to *do*?

It is God's goal for us to live a life of purpose. In order to do this we sometimes have to be pushed. This can be uncomfortable but God does this for our benefit. This pressure propels us to become better people so that we can live better lives. Similar to when a mother eagle stirs the nest because she knows her children are ready to fly. She knows that if she allows her eaglets to stay at the stage they are in for too long, they will get comfortable and miss the boundless sights of the sky that awaits them. Likewise, God doesn't want us to miss out on the extraordinary opportunities that He has for our lives. So, He will stir our nests, allowing discomfort to get us to move to from one level to the next. As we trust Him and take leaps of faith, He transforms us from being self-centered to being Christ-centered hearers and doers.

CHAPTER 4

ENGAGE IN THE PROCESS

Many times, we mistake who we are for what we do. They are not the same thing. Entrepreneur, Speaker, Breakthrough Strategist are simply titles that I hold because they describe what I do, but that is not to be confused with my true identity. I *am* always a child of God.

God created us to reflect his glory and when we seek our identity in anything else outside of him, we miss out on unlocking our full potential and making His name great on earth. Society tries to tempt us into finding our identity in everything outside of God. They want us to live up to their standards oppose to living up to the standards of the God that created us. Knowing who we are in Christ is the answer to living a happy and fulfilling life and to obtaining everything we spend our entire lives trying to achieve. Where are you tempted to find your identity? Is it in your relationship status? Your church? Your career? The number of degrees you have? Your social status?

Your identity can't be found in any of those things. You have to go to the source, which is God. In His word is where we find our true selves and his perfect plans for our lives. This requires a pursuit. We get revelation about our identity when we read God's word. Through prayer we receive affirmation about who we are in Christ and the actions we should take. And when we worship, we are celebrating who He is in relationship to who we are. These are some of the spiritual building blocks that help us discover our identity.

If we place our identity in anything other than God, a relationship, our financial status, our spouse, our children it will eventually become problematic because all of these things change. That is why the Bible says this in 2nd Corinthians 4:18, "so we fix our eyes not on what is seen, but on what is unseen, since what is seen is temporary, but what is unseen is eternal."

When we focus on the invisible we can do the impossible. God is solid. He won't just randomly switch up on you. "He is the same yesterday, today and forever" (Hebrews 13:8).

This is good news! When the world is constantly changing, we can find our security in Christ.

When we really understand our identity in Christ and encompass all that we are — in Him, it changes everything about our lives. It changes the way we think and live. And It is only when we have *real* fellowship with Him that we can discover the truth about who we really are and live a completely successful life.

True Identity

I don't know about you but discovering my identity in Christ was one of those things that I really struggled with. I had experienced so many heartbreaks and painful situations throughout my life and it all made me feel worthless. I don't know if you can relate. So, when I first started going to church and hearing about how valuable I was in Christ, it was a little hard to believe.

I think many of us understand that our identity is found in Christ on some level, but it's difficult for us to receive it and believe that what he says about us in His word, is true. The challenges we've faced and the things that people have said that have hurt us can be louder than what is said about us in God's word. I know that this was true for me. I didn't have very much confidence. And the thing about it is when you don't understand who you are, you don't understand where you belong. You are unsure of what you should be doing next or where you should be going. And as a result, you end up settling for a lot less than God's best in your life. Deep down, I knew that I didn't want to live an average, ordinary or mediocre life. I wanted to make my mark on the world. I wanted to make a difference. I think we all do. But sometimes life gets the best of us and we find ourselves settling out of fear, doubt, insecurities and heart wounds. I literally had to brainwash myself with the word of God. Sounds a little bit over-the-top, right? But it's true. When I first started to find out about what was available to me through my identity in Christ— I wanted it. That is the thing about breaking free. You've got to want it. I mean *really* want it. I'll talk to you about that more later in the book. But anyway, I had to count all past sources of my confidence and identity as worthless and choose to believe that what God said about me was true. So do you! When I finally decided to start walking in the truth of God's word, my life changed drastically for the better. My life has never been the same.

But, I had to be willing to open myself to God and give him my pain, my problems and the old perceptions I had about myself. The thing about God is that you must give up your life, to get a life. Remember when that was a popular phrase? Get a life! Okay, well maybe some of you do and some of you don't, but either way, you can get one. Not just a mediocre one, but a fabulous one, if you're willing to let him in. I mean *all* the way in.

Think about an olive seed for a moment, it doesn't sit in a bag and become a full-grown 30-foot olive tree overnight, does it? No, that olive seed must fall in the ground and die. Then it needs to break through the soil, grow roots, and find nutrients to feed on. It needs to be watered and get sunlight. It is just then that you see a bud coming out, then a leaf pops up, and eventually the tree begins to grow.

This is true of an olive seed in process to become an Olive tree. The same is true for the process God has for you to become who He called you to be.

There are so many characters in the Bible that God took through a radical transformation, but let's talk about Gideon for minute. The mighty warrior we also see depicted in the Hollywood movie "300." However, the story in the Bible didn't go quite as it did on the screen.

The whole story of Gideon illustrates the concept of us unlocking our full potential and going from victim to victor perfectly. Gideon goes from being weak to being a warrior. He discovers his true identity through his authentic connection with God — His willingness to *"keep it real"* about his limitations. God affirmed him until his faith was strong enough to take action and to obey His voice. Gideon ended up being overwhelmingly victorious and everyone around him benefited. This is what God wants for all of us. He wants the success of our lives to spill over and improve the quality of life for those around us. In order for us to do this, we must be willing to let go of who we "think" we are and embrace our true identity in Christ.

Let's look at Gideon's story *(**Judges 6 - 8**)*

Gideon was threshing out wheat in a hidden place, when the Angel of the Lord appeared, sat down under and oak tree and said to him *"The Lord is with you, you mighty warrior."*

Gideon replied, *"Pardon me, my lord, but if the Lord is with us, why has all this happened to us? Where are all his wonders that our ancestors told us about when they said, 'Did not the Lord bring us up out of Egypt?' But now the Lord has abandoned us and given us into the hand of Midian."*

So, basically Gideon responds to the Angel of the Lord with fear and unbelief like "Hold up Angel of The Lord! First of all, are you talking to me? Do you know the situation me and my people are in?" Oh... and by the way you're a little late God. Where is all the stuff you promised me? I've been waiting for you to do some supernatural stuff around here for years!

The Lord faced Gideon and said *"Go in the strength you have and save Israel out of Midian's hand. Am I not sending you?"*

Gideon was like, "Wait, What strength?" "Didn't you hear what I just said?"

And then He responds to God again. But this time not just with his fears and unbelief, but also from the place of his insecurities. *"Pardon me, my lord, but how can I save Israel? My clan is the weakest in Manasseh, and I am the least in my family."*

Side Note: I hope you don't mind, I am giving you the "Break Free Version" of this story, but I encourage you to read it for yourself when you can make the time.

Ok so back to Gideon! He was like *Look, I told you. I am the weakest link around here, can't you just get someone else to do this?"*

Have you ever felt like that with God? Responding to His instructions with your fears, doubts, and insecurities?

Gideon goes back and forth with God repeatedly trying to convince Him that he is not the man for the job, but God kept on affirming his identity and encouraging him.

God says to Gideon: I'll be with you. Believe Me. You'll defeat your enemies.

And then, after all that, Gideon still asks God for a sign. A sign! Can you believe this guy? Of course, you can! I'm sure that you have asked God for a sign at least once or twice in your life when whatever He asks you to do seems totally crazy.

But anyway, God was faithful to respond.

This is how it played out. Gideon goes and prepares a sacred meal to bring back as a gift to the Angel of The Lord. God took the tip of a stick, touched the meal and set it on fire. God was pretty much like, 'You wanted a sign, here's a sign!' but that still wasn't enough to convince Gideon or to secure His identity or confidence in Christ. I could almost hear him saying, "Wow God, that was amazing, but I'm still not really sure if you are talking to me. I don't believe I'm capable of doing what you are asking me to do. So, Gideon asked God to be patient with him and asked for *another* sign. And guess what? God did it!

After the first sign, when God set that stick a blaze, I would have been like "Ok God! Where do I sign?" But I guess Gideon needed a little more confirmation.

Two signs Gideon asked for - Not one, but two and God was faithful to answer him both times.

You know why? Because God is good! He is graceful, patient, loving, and kind! Trusting God's faithfulness drives out our fears. He isn't concerned with our problems and false perceptions, He is only concerned with us maximizing our potential and fulfilling our purpose on earth. In him, **you are enough and you have everything you need right now to break free and be unstoppable.**

God gave Gideon all the signs he needed to step out on faith. He loved him through his fears, doubts, and insecurities. I think we can all relate to His story because there are times when we are discouraged and it is hard for us to move forward in life. In our fellowship with God, we can find strength for our struggles and overcome victoriously just like Gideon.

God just wants us to believe.

God had already told Gideon:
He was chosen.
He was a warrior.
He was strong.
He was victorious.

But, Gideon was so focused on himself and who he thought he was, that he really couldn't receive God's truth about his identity. Sometimes, our voice or the voices around us are so loud that we end up tuning God out. Unintentionally, we become self-centered. The world around us is built to exalt "the self! Selfies, Facebook, Instagram, Twitter, and television. Everything in society is designed to make us focus on ourselves.

Sometimes we can get so caught up on who the world says we are or are not - that we miss God when He shows up to tell us who we were made to be.

What I love about this story is that every time Gideon disqualified himself, God would come back and remind him that he was already qualified. God doesn't call the qualified, He qualifies the called!

The same way God worked with Gideon, He will work with you. I encourage you to *"keep it real"* with God and let His love and infinite power that works within us, upgrade your self-perception and your pursuit of God's best for your life.

Gideon eventually trusted God and acted. He started preparing for the battle. And after all the he had been through, God comes and says something unexpected. He looked at Gideon's already outnumbered army and says, "That's way too many men. Plus, some of them will take credit for what I am about to do through you and forget about me."

God told Gideon to get rid of the fearful and suspect fighters.

So, Gideon got rid of some of the men but still God thought he had too many. The Lord gave him some more instructions to weed out his crew and he obeyed. Gideon got down to 300 men.

Gideon must have been freaking out by now. He was probably thinking, "God how did we go from 32,000 to 300 men?"

At that very moment, God gave him the strategy to win the battle — "Get up and go down to the camp. I've given it to you. If you have any doubts about going down, go down with your armor bearer; when you hear what they're saying, you'll be bold and confident."

I love this! God is still working with Gideon because He knows that he is still a little scared. Gideon eventually followed God's instructions. And even though his army was outnumbered, they still won the battle.

The Bible says that Gideon divided his army into three companies and then each company took a strategic position to surround the enemy's camp. After that, the three hundred men blew their trumpets and smashed the jars on top of their torches to uncover the fire and make noise. It was in that exact moment that God aimed each Midianites sword against his companion, all over the camp. Gideon's enemies ran for their lives.

Gideon's army won the battle by raising torches, breaking jars, and blowing trumpets. Can you believe it? Because we all know that this is how you win battles...right? Of course not! Let's be honest! God's request was totally crazy!

But it doesn't matter how crazy God's instructions are, because He will always come through for you. God is a promise keeper. Your job is not to worry about the how, your job is to listen for God's voice and obey.

In some area of your life you might be feeling the way Gideon did. I don't know what area it is — ministry, business, school, or relationships. But whatever it is God just wants you to engage in the process. To offer yourself. To fully participate in His plans and purposes for your life.

If you are reading this now and feel like you haven't fully or every really committed yourself to God and His plans for your life, then hurry up and turn to the last page of this book and say that prayer. If you already have a relationship with God, then I encourage you to keep walking by faith. Engage in the process of discovering the next dimension of your identity and do whatever God is telling you to do next.

I can relate to Gideon so much. God has called me to wear many hats among multiple industries. Let's be clear — that was not my plan! I went to college and I wanted to work a job! A 9-5. An administrative position in the arts sounded lovely. It sounded safe. I had no intentions of ever being an entrepreneur or doing any of the things that I am doing now, including writing this book! God kept on pushing me out of my comfort zone. Every time I found myself secure in an industry or in a role, he would open a door and the next thing you know, I would be learning something new and doing something else. To some, this might sound exhilarating and fulfilling, but for me it was terrifying. Each new opportunity came with its own insecurities and challenges.

For example, the first big jump, was when he took me from grad school into the working world. After I interviewed for a job where I could comfortably sit behind a desk, they offered me a position, working with youth and traveling all over the city. It wasn't enough money, so I did acting gigs and worked side jobs to pay the bills.

From working with youth, I went on to facilitating professional development workshops with adults, but I didn't know what to wear or what to say. The culture was totally different from when I was in a classroom jumping on top of desks, making animal noises, and leading improvisation games. I was insecure about talking to adults because I had only ever spoken to youth.

From there, I became a contractor with the school system. I really had to step my game up then because I didn't know anything about business. This was really when I was like God: Ok, what are you doing with my life? Remember, I have a theater degree. Why am I in-front of a room full of teachers talking to them about how to help students learn?

The leaps of faith continued, and I eventually started my own business and ministry, and it keeps going on from there. Like Gideon, I never once felt qualified for anything that God was telling me to do.

God listens, and He longs to give us His best. But, we need to be willing to endure the process required to enjoy the abundant life He has for us. **You must be willing to break free from where you came from in order to embrace your future.**

Don't get discouraged or give up when God interrupts your life to activate who you *really* are and to develop your character. He loves you and he is only trying to help you get form where you are to where you both want you to be.

Engage In Your Process: Real Talk

1 John 4:4 New International Version (NIV)
You, dear children, are from God and have overcome them,

because the one who is in you is greater than the one who is in the world.

That is the truth for all of us. The bible tells us that we are greater in Christ then we are in ourselves. Our humanity is limited, but in Christ we are unlimited and have access to an infinite realm of possibilities. It is only when we choose to be hidden in Christ, that our lives will ever be seen.

When I say hidden in Christ, I don't mean hiding behind him. Sometimes, it can be easy to hide behind our faith. Using our spiritual principles and religious jargon to mask our lack of action. That is not this! I am talking about really and truly engaging in an intimate, authentic connection with God.

A relationship that is much deeper than rigidly following religious principles or quoting our favorite church-isms. It is only when we take the time to build our relationships with him and allow ourselves to be fully invested that we will ever know God —for real and know ourselves.

It's just like friendship. There are levels to it. Your best friends are the people in your life that you know and who know you the best. Then you have friends that you have compartmentalized. Meaning, you have "church friends" or you have "work friends". You care for these individuals too, but you only hang out with him when you are in those locations. So, they have limited knowledge about you and your life. And you have limited knowledge about them too. We must be careful not to do this with God. We cannot compartmentalize Him. He does not go in our box. If you put him in one, you will miss out on the best part of the relationship.

For example, only fellowshipping with him when you are in crises or only on Wednesday when you meet with your small group at church or when you talk to that one friend — you will miss out on all that he is. If you have God in a box, take him out! That is the only way that you will ever be able to engage in the process of discovering your full potential.

If you are hearing this for the first time, it may seem weird or wrong. But sometimes we do "wrong" so long that it feels right. When you know God, and are confident in his love you will be able to trust him. I mean really trust him. Not just when everything in your life is going great, but when the storms of life try to take you out! That is the thing about God. **We must trust Him when we can't trace Him.**

That is what it means to walk by faith and not by sight. It is only then that we can receive God's best for our lives and be a tremendous blessing to others. So, be like Gideon. Keep it real with God, but remember you must also be willing to *keep it real* with yourself.

CHAPTER 5

TRANSFORM YOUR THINKING

Before we enter this chapter, there are three foundational scriptures I want you to remember.

Romans 12:2 New International Version (NIV)
Do not conform to the pattern of this world, but be transformed by the renewing of your mind. Then you will be able to test and approve what God's will is—his good, pleasing and perfect will.

Proverbs 23:7 King James Version (KJV)
For as he thinketh in his heart, so is he: Eat and drink, saith he to thee; but his heart is not with thee.

Proverbs 4:23 New International Version (NIV)
Above all else guard your heart, for everything you do flows from it.

Train Your Thinking

Now that you have read them, let's dig deep into each one of them. The Bible says "be transformed by the renewing of your mind. Then you will be able to test and approve what God's will is—his good, pleasing and perfect will". So, when we talk about training our thinking, we are talking about managing our thought life. God knows that the key to a successful life is mind renewal.

Some people believe that the key is in our heart, when the reality is that our thoughts are what nurtures our hearts. This means that whatever we think, informs our feelings, and furthermore, our decisions.

The Bible says in Proverbs 23:7 that as a man thinks in his heart so is he. God is letting us know that we think in our heart. He's letting us know that our minds and our hearts are two of our most crucial components and that they are connected. So, that's where our attention needs to be, to what's coming into our minds and what's going into our hearts.

The Bible also says that out of our heart flow the issues of life. So, whatever we are experiencing in our minds and hearts, we can be sure to see manifested in our lives.

We need to tend to our minds like we would tend to a garden. We must be diligent about plucking out our negative thoughts and thought patterns like weeds. The wrong thoughts produce chaos and will eventually jeopardize our harvest, and this could totally derail us emotionally and otherwise, leading us into taking actions that we wouldn't do if we had better thoughts or managed our thoughts in life in a healthier manner. Plucking out the weeds in our mind is an ongoing process because our minds require daily maintenance.

In a garden full of weeds, would you be able to see much fruit or flowers? No, Right? The same is true for our lives. If our mind is cluttered with negative thoughts, it will be impossible to inherit the promises of God in our lives. Transformed thinking is the beginning of transformed living.

We literally must arrest our thoughts and bring them under the submission of God's word. If we don't, we risk our thought life becoming disorderly and potentially destructive, depending on what you are thinking about all the time.

I know this may sound unusual, but we must become fully aware of what we're thinking about. You must deliberately ask yourself, is this thought in agreement with God's word or is it contradictory? Once we answer that question, then we can decide to embrace or reject that thought.

Just like a personal trainer has his or her clients exercise repeatedly to whip their body into shape, we must do the same thing with our minds. You must resist, reject, and replace all thoughts that are not in alignment with the highest truth concerning your identity and your life. The highest truth for both of those is the Word of God. That is one of the reasons why we should all read the Word of God often, that is the only and most effective way to replace the wrong information with righteous information.

Just like a body out of shape endures health issues and complications as years go by, if our mind is out of shape, severe consequences will begin to manifest in our lives. Thoughts of fear will lead to failure. For example, a fear of being broke will limit your ability to produce more income. We need to remember this and always keep that in our mind. So, we don't ever settle for living a mediocre life.

Managing your thoughts may seem tedious, but it is crucial to your success and living a happy, fulfilling, and prosperous life. It is something you practice and repeat every day. Over time, your thinking will begin to transform. You will grow and develop a mind of flourishing thoughts, just like a garden grows and develops beautiful flowers. The entire process starts with us reading the Word of God. Trust me, this is where it all begins. God will meet you where you are. You just have to get started!

The Word Works

"For the word of God is alive and active. Sharper than any double-edged sword, it penetrates even to dividing soul and spirit, joints and marrow; it judges the thoughts and attitudes of the heart" (Hebrews 4:12).

The Word of God is powerful! It is living just like the food we eat, as strange comparison, but hear me out! Think of the food that we eat on a daily basis; the nutrients do not need instructions from us on where to go within our bodies or how to nurture us. They already know what to do. The Word of God works in the same way. It already knows what to do on the inside of us once we really accept it and allow it to take root. When we allow God's Word to drop down from our minds into our hearts, it will begin to transform us and everything about our lives.

"Night and day, whether he sleeps or gets up, the seed sprouts and grows, though he does not know how" (Mark 4:27).

In verse 27, the farmer plants the seeds, but the growth comes from the Lord. So, he does his part and goes to bed, then God comes in and does what only He can do.

Your part is to read the Bible, and the renewal comes from the Lord.

When I was in college, I took a Bible with me, but I had never really opened it up. The church I went to when I was younger was a good church, but they never really taught me about the Power of God or about His supernatural ability. It was more just that God loves you and we love God. End of story. We never talked about miracles, never talked about how the Word of God has the power to impact our finances and the way we live or even about its power to heal our bodies. I didn't know any of that, all I knew was that you were supposed to love God and that God loves us.

I grew up thinking and believing only that. Hear me out, God's love is true, it is the biggest most important thing in the Bible. Believing this one truth is not bad, but that's not the entire truth about God. There are more aspects to His character than just His love. He is almighty and powerful. And He is always able to perform the most amazing miracles in our lives to show us that He is the truth, the way and the life (John

14:6).

I learn more about God every time I pick up my Bible and we all do. Just like any relationship you have, you learn more about the person as you spend time with them.

Bringing it back to what I was talking about, I didn't really start reading my Bible until I was in college. It all started on one terrible evening when I was all alone in a friend's apartment, as everyone else had gone home for Christmas break.

I had just broken up with my boyfriend at the time. And that was not only heartbreaking but very inconvenient. I lived two trains and one bus away from my college campus, and I used to stay at his apartment whenever I had night classes. Now, where was I going to stay? How was I going to manage my schedule?

Fortunately, one of my girlfriends that lived in his same building offered me to stay with her and that is how I ended up at her apartment during Christmas break.

I was all alone, heartbroken, laying on an air mattress in her living room, eating a frozen pizza I prepared in her oven as my dinner, and crying my eyes out.

What am I doing with my life?

I am in college, I have a dead-end job that barely pays my bills, I have no boyfriend, my family is miles away, and I am here crashing in a friend's living room.

Suddenly, I saw my Bible, sitting on a radiator across the room, along with some clothes and jewelry. I had taken it with me to college and up to that point, I had never read it. But that night something happened and for the first time I picked it up and opened it. I remember it landed on Ephesians, I know because I remember reading about the possibility of my heart being flooded with light, and that stuck with me.

Ephesians 1:18 New Living Translation (NLT)
I pray that your hearts will be flooded with light so that you can understand the confident hope he has given to those he called—his holy people who are his rich and glorious inheritance.

Now, let me make something clear before I move on, although these holidays often make people more sensitive to God related things, I know it was the Spirit of God who drew me to pick up my Bible that night. It wasn't like my Bible was something that I carried with me everywhere.

But something told me to get up, go over, and start reading the Bible. So, I did, and that's what started my whole walk with God.

I didn't go to church, it was just opening that book, the only book that can save lives.

As I began to read it something started to happen to me although I wasn't aware of it at the time. I didn't really understand it but the Holy Spirit was teaching me new things every day. Next thing you know I'm journaling, I'm writing down scriptures. It wasn't until years after that I found myself back in a church, but I was walking with God as a part of my daily routine.

What I'm trying to explain is that the Word of God started to transform my mind and heart. It started to draw me in, it began to change me day by day, and it made me curious and thirsty for more. How did all of this happen? It happened without me doing anything but reading His Word. It was not something I planned, it was His love that drew me in. As I continued to read and allowed it to direct, mold, shape, and change me, my life began to transform. I went from no car, to having a car. Hourly side jobs became secure contract after contract. I went from depressed to full of joy. Overdrawn accounts to overflowing accounts, and this was all happening because of reading God's Word. Reading it and allowing it to shape and form a new reality, God's best. This is what he wants to do for you as well. You may already have a lot of what I mentioned in your own life, but we all need something. Maybe you need better health, you want a husband, you need more peace and joy, or success for your children. Whatever it is, it can be found in the living Word of God.

More often than not, people say things like 'I don't think God talks to me', or 'how do I hear His voice?' God can speak directly to you, but his voice is also His Word. The more you are in His Word, the more you can begin to recognize his voice. If you have His Word and you have His voice, then you have Him. The Word is God. If you have the Word, you have God. Meaning, He is on the scene. He has arrived in all his splendor, glory, and power.

"In the beginning was the Word, and the Word was with God, and the Word was God" (John 1:1).

If you ask me, I never felt ready to meet with God. I wasn't even aware that I needed Him. But as I began to read my Bible, my heart softened, and the next thing you know I started praying and worshiping God.

The Bible says, draw near to God and He will draw near to you. *"Come near to God and he will come near to you. Wash your hands, you sinners, and purify your hearts, you double-minded" (James 4:8).*

And that is exactly what I began to do. The rest flowed from that place of intimacy. It didn't require a big plan on my part to woe God, so He would come and seek me. All it took was a little disposition to read His word, one day at a time.

Meditate Until It Breaks

We are all living out of a blueprint. Just like the house or building you are living in was created from one. Our backgrounds, conversations, experiences, heartbreaks, achievements, etc.; draws that blueprint in our hearts, what we listen to, what we watch. It all contributes to building that blueprint. Our blueprints also get shaped by our thoughts. That is why it is so important to manage our thinking. When we meditate God's word, it penetrates our hearts and eventually manifests in our lives.

Understanding your blueprint will help you discover where and why you're stuck. It will also help you find out why you're not experiencing certain results in your life. Imagine the blueprint for a house. If the blueprint has no windows, the house will have no windows. The same is true for our lives. The word of God is our master blueprint. Our lives should mirror the scriptures. And to build a storm-resistant life we must meditate on God's Word.

Meditating is more than just reading. To meditate means that you're rehearsing the Word of God repeatedly in your mind; you're getting it ingrained in your heart and speech. You are keeping it at the center of your life.

Let's break it down, beginning with the actual definition in the dictionary:

To meditate: think deeply or focus one's mind, often in silence, for religious or spiritual purposes and as a method of relaxation.

So, to meditate means to really give your full attention to something and then think about it repeatedly. To ponder about it and extract meaning.

Meditation Brings Revelation.

When we meditate we reconstruct our minds to match God's word. And as we speak his word we will see the promises of God manifested in our lives.

The Bible says in *Joshua 1:8 New International Version (NIV): Keep this Book of the Law always on your lips; meditate on it day and night, so that you may be careful to do everything written in it. Then you will be prosperous and successful.*

It is only when we meditate the Word of God and do what it says that we will thrive beyond our wildest imagination.

If You Can Shape It in Your Mind, You Can See It in Your Life.

For example, let's say your thoughts prior to meditating the Word of God were centered around your desire for a steadier flow of clientele, as an entrepreneur. But after meditating scriptures that promise you increase, you now know how to combat your old way of thinking and can receive revelation pertaining to the strategy required to optimize your business.

Here's another example. Something I saw in my own life was money. I was very bad at managing money. I would make money and then overspend. This is when I saw the creative power of God's Word work in my life. I didn't realize back then that this came from a compromised blueprint I was subconsciously following. I had a fear of running out of money or that I was unable to make enough. It came from my past failure of mismanagement and having small jobs where I was not paid much at all and had to ask to borrow money to pay my rent and anything else I was behind on. But, I got ahold of God's word and found scriptures like:

Psalm 112:3 New International Version (NIV)
Wealth and riches are in their houses, and their righteousness endures forever.

Deuteronomy 8:18 New International Version (NIV)
But remember the LORD your God, for it is he who gives you the ability to produce wealth, and so confirms his covenant, which he swore to your ancestors, as it is today.

Psalm 115:14 New International Version (NIV)
May the LORD cause you to flourish, both you and your children.

Suddenly, things began to happen. God began to give me a revelation about money, a deeper revelation about giving and my financial habits. Over time, I started being more diligent about my spending, giving more, and taking actions that were congruent with the revelation I was receiving from the scriptures. It started to bring more wealth into my life in a variety of ways. Occupational contracts, I'd receive special discounts in stores, cheaper flights, free cell phones, etc. There were different ways that the Lord began to show me prosperity. It was truly supernatural. I knew it was Him, and it all started with meditating on the word.

I encourage you to remain diligent as you apply the word of God to your life. Replacing facts with God's truth. The fact was that I was broke, but God's word promised me wealth and riches. You won't know that you're being deceived, unless you read God's word.

You will not catch everything from the start, but it will start to make more sense as time passes by and you continue to read it.

It's like someone teaching you a dance, they will teach you the steps repeatedly, but unless dance is an area you're gifted in, you're not going to pick up dance on the first try, you may pick it up on the 3rd or 4th some people may pick it up on the 14th or 15th time, but it depends on the person's familiarity with dance.

Our willingness to be coachable determines how much and how fast we learn.

When you meditate on the Word of God, it begins to align you with the truth about who you really are in Christ, which is the best possible version of you versus the person you may think you are right now.

When you meditate on the Word of God, you grow and you change from the inside out. Then, as a result, you start to attract different people, new opportunities, and that process just keeps going on and on.

The more you meditate and allow the Word of God to transform you from the inside out, the more you will begin to pick up the rhythm of God's purposes for your life. The more we read and listen to his word, the more we become like Him, the closer we get to becoming everything that he has created us to be.

When we slow down and take time to read God's Word to transform our thinking, incredible things can happen.

Resist, Reject, Replace

2 Corinthians 10:5 New International Version (NIV)
We demolish arguments and every pretension that sets itself up against the knowledge of God, and we take captive every thought to make it obedient to Christ.

When thoughts that oppose God's word enter your mind, you must do what the Word says, "casting down every high thought that exalts itself against the knowledge of God". This is where we move into being a doer of the Word which I mentioned before.

If you believe, read, meditate, and speak the word it will begin to transform you, I guarantee it but if you don't cast down negative thoughts and those that oppose God's word, your thinking will not fully transform.

Reading, meditating and speaking the word of God are all helpful and positively influential. They work to transform your thinking in a comprehensive way. However, I notice in my life that reading the Word or just saying it out loud is not enough if I don't fight back when the enemy shoots his fiery darts into my psyche'. I can't go where God is trying to take me. My negative thinking begins to take over and move me out of God's will and ways. It pushes me away from my purpose and God's best. I end up being led astray and end up off track or less productive. Over time from not resisting, rejecting, or replacing my negative thinking with the word of God. This increased the challenges, frustrations, and distractions that I experienced in life.

We've got to let the enemy know we mean business! It's like counter-culture, you can't operate a business well, with two opposites, and two contrary ways of doing things. Meditating on God's word is an entirely new way of thinking — that is not like the world. For example, think about the culture of these two restaurants, McDonald's and Taco Bell. Their approaches are totally different. Their menus are not the same, one with burgers and fries, and the other tacos with nachos. Trying to have both in one place would be very conflicting for both businesses as well as their customers. These two businesses up against each other like that is a great example of what happens in our thought life when we don't resist, reject and replace our carnal thinking with the word of God.

If both of those operations were under the same roof, using the same equipment, how well do you think they would function?

If we don't consistently cast down our negative thoughts, our minds cannot be renewed.

It is also a matter of perception. For example, if you lose weight, but you keep thinking that you are overweight, every day, you will live your life out of that perception. The same with the Word of God. If you read you are loved and accepted, but you keep thinking that you are rejected, you will live your life out of that misconception. You are the gatekeeper of your thought life. You get to decide what comes in, but you are also in charge of what to keep out!

Here's the thing, when you cast down negative thoughts, you are breaking your agreement with them. When you don't, you end up living in a disillusioned agreement with them.

Let's be honest, you can't become all that God's called you to be when you're agreeing with the culture of Satan. Some people think it's not that serious, but it is, unless we renew our minds to God's Word, there is no way to reach our full potential, live out our purpose, or receive God's best in our lives. You can't defeat the devil and the fiery darts that he shoots into your mind alone. Your strength is not enough. Only the power of God and His word are a match for Satan. Don't ever forget that!

One thing I've noticed though, is that the more I enthusiastically and diligently reach towards the plans and purposes that God has for my life, the less resisting, rejecting, and replacing I do!

So, resist, reject and replace...but most importantly REACH.

Crack The Code

Sometimes people self-sabotage their success without even knowing it because they are living out of undetected thought and behavioral patterns. As a result, they end up attracting the very situations they said they didn't want. And one of the hardest things to do is to bring yourself up to where God is calling your to be, rather than staying where you are, with what is comfortable or where you came from. If we recognize that we are getting results that we are not happy with in our lives, businesses, relationships or whatever the case might be, we need to Crack the Code! We must be willing to discover why we keep finding ourselves in the same situations repeatedly. This is easier said, then done.

For example, you're single and you haven't been asked on a date in years, you keep getting stuck at a certain amount of income or you can't seem to attract or keep enough clients to sustain your business.

Whatever the pattern is that you keep bumping into in your business, relationships or in your life — it is critical to your success that you crack the code. You must consider the reason for why it keeps happening. Search for the common denominators.

We should not be so naive and become so caught up on our performance or perfections, that we forget to consider ourselves as a part of the problem. Oh! And the solution, also. If we are not careful to dig deeper this could turn into us acting better than we are living. I believe this happens to everybody at some point, but we can't let it go on forever. We need to crack the code! The consequences of living or doing business with these undetected patterns are too expensive. They will cost you time, energy, relationships and money. I'll give you an example of myself.

My business mentor was the one that clued me in on this when I was frustrated for the thousandth time about my friends not coming through for me. I met with her, while I was out of town. During a quick break, I had some time alone and I spoke with some of my friends that promised they were going to come see me before I left, but during our conversation they expressed that they could no longer come. All I heard was excuses because in my mind, if they really wanted to see me, they would have made it happen. When I met back with my mentor, after our break was over, she said, what happened to you? I was wearing the disappointment and I didn't even know it.

I told her the story and she asked me if my friends had disappointed me like this before. I said yes. She explained to me that a very small percentage of people do what they say and that if I choose to break down every time people fell short or failed to meet my expectations, that I was going to spend a majority of my life being disappointed.

I had to eliminate that way of thinking because it triggered frustration that led to old behavioral patterns that I desperately needed to break. She told me that I needed to manage my expectations. I had never done this before. She explained to me that their unwillingness to come see me didn't mean that they didn't love me, or that they were bad people, but that if I made it mean that — then it would. She helped me understand that there could have been multiple reasons for their un-willingness to show up. She challenged me to see the situation from their perspective and not just my own.

For years, I had been holding on to the disappointment of people not doing what they said they were going to do for me. I had to realize that in some cases I had lofty, expectations of how people should act and treat me. This was a barrier to me being able to love people unconditionally. The offense I would take in my heart would lead to bitterness when they didn't meet those expectations.

I realized that I was subconsciously trying to make people prove that they loved me. In situations like these there are so many perspectives we can take. The truth in my situation was that those friends did love me, but they were not willing to make that level of sacrifice to get me from across town. Some people will do what they say, and some will not. Some friends will come get you in the middle of rush hour and some will not, but it doesn't necessarily mean they don't love you, or me, or that we should take our love away from them, or that we should make it mean something about our value. Instead of focusing on the behaviors of others when we are disappointed, upset or living with less desirable results, we should reflect on our own mindsets and beliefs. This is the only way that we will ever learn, progress and unlock our full potential. We need to crack the code so that we can fully embrace the gifts that God has for us in our friendships, families, finances and in our lives.

After that situation, I did some more reflecting and later God reveled to me that I needed to spend more time in his word building a correct self-image. So, I did. And I applied my revelation to many other areas of my life. When we crack the code in one area of our life it can give us keys to unlock other doors and not just for ourselves, but for others. So, I encourage you to spend some quiet time with God and to let him reveal any thought patterns that may be preventing you from going to that next level in your life, relationships or business.

Talk to God and then...Crack the code!

Put It into Practice

Renewing our minds is a process; and it is ongoing. There is a direct correlation between our faith, our relationship with God, our willingness to endure the process of transforming our thinking, and the fruits we bear.

As you embark upon the journey of upgrading your thought life, you must be patient with yourself. You must also allow yourself to be held accountable. Accountability is a catalyst to breakthrough. In my life, I have given certain people permission to hold me accountable. These people keep me in check. If I begin to complain or talk negatively, they lovingly correct me, encourage me, then remind me to move my speech into the opposite direction. When they do this, it is slightly irritating, to be honest, but then I am reminded to reflect and redirect my thinking. People will not just do this for you because most are not doing it for themselves, but if you have somebody that you love and trust, ask them to help you be accountable. It will give you a sense of belonging and remind you that you are not alone. This can ignite internal motivation that can fuel you further, faster in your transformational thinking process. It will also turn your intention into an agreement. And those agreements will turn into a "must do" action.

Accountability separates the dreamers from the doers. Having it communicates that you care enough about your future to account for the actions you take in your daily life.

I suggest reaching out for accountability in any area of your life — not just your thinking — that you want to see a breakthrough. Find somebody who is developed in that area and get to work alongside them, listen to what they say and learn from their experience. How do they move on stuff when they're afraid? How do they manage their thought life? Whatever "it" is - discover it.

Set yourself up for success.

Don't put yourself in compromising situations that will tempt or trigger you into old ways of thinking or negative thought patterns. For example, if you are friends with a negative Nancy and she is complaining all the time, you may have to limit your time and conversations with her.

Rotten fruit is easy to spot. When you eat the rotten fruit of other's speech, attitudes, actions and behaviors, it's likely to produce the same in you. That is why it is important to be selective about what we watch, listen, and expose ourselves to. Whatever we take in daily affects our thoughts.

The Bible says this in *Mark 4:24 New International Version* (NIV) *24 "Consider carefully what you hear,"* he continued. *"With the measure you use, it will be measured to you—and even more.*

Some people can't listen to certain kinds of music, if they listen to a certain genre of songs for too long they are ready to pop, lock and drop something! I hope you know what I mean by that. You must know what works for you and what doesn't. You have to know your limits. You need to know, if that song, television show, conversation, hanging out with that one person or whatever it is, if it's constructing or destructing?

Whatever you feed will lead.

So, if you don't want to live a fearful life, don't fill your mind with things that make you worry. Remember, you are the gatekeeper of your thought life!

Maybe you have heard this before.

Our thoughts become our words, our words become our actions, our actions become our habits, and our habits determine our lives.

It all starts with our thoughts. The decision to make God's word true in our lives. For real. Not the truth that we simply let sit on our night stand, but the truth that we read, meditate and let live in our hearts.

"I will take your stony heart and I will give you a heart of flesh"
(Ezekiel 36:26).

In chapter one, I talked about being guarded and how being guarded leads to our hearts being hard. If our hearts are hard, not much of anything will be able to get through it. For us to be led by those that God has entrusted us with, or to be led by God directly, we must be willing to be open. Sometimes, our hearts get hard because of life's challenge's and the seed, that is the Word of God, gets repelled or will not take root. We need our hearts to be softened to believe that what God says about us is true. The word can help us do that!

We must all practice the concepts that have been mentioned in this chapter if we what to break free and stay free in all areas of our lives.

We must master the art of tracking and training our thinking.

Remember, resist, reject, and replace! We can't do just one or two of these. We must do all three.

It's like trying to have a peanut butter and jelly sandwich, with no peanut butter, no jelly, and no bread. The three ingredients become a sandwich when assembled together, not before.

It works like a system similar to working out and not eating right, you're not going to be as fit as you want to be unless you get that eating down pact. They even say 80% is eating and 20% exercising. So, in our spiritual life, God is the gym you go to work out your faith and the Bible is the good food you eat to stay healthy. But you know, the gym and the food thing, won't work unless you *work* them. They are always there, available, waiting on you but it is you who needs to take the actions.

After you practice for a while, it will become more automatic, you will gain new muscle memory in your mind. Just like all other things that you learned and now do naturally, like brushing your teeth. You don't have to be reminded about the benefits of it every day. For you, it's a no brainer, you simply do it. You do it because it's a habit, you already know it's necessary for your hygiene.

Well, tracking and training your thinking is part of your spiritual health routine, and you must practice it every day, until it becomes as natural as brushing your teeth. Get ready to smile!

CHAPTER 6

MANAGE YOUR MOUTH

G rowing up, I'm sure you heard this rhyme at least once or twice, "Sticks and stones may break my bones, but words can never hurt me"

The devil is a liar! Words do hurt! But the good news is, they can also be used to heal.

The Bible says in Proverbs 30:32, *"if thou hast thought evil, lay thine hand upon thy mouth."* This is because whatever you are thinking is probably just seconds away from coming out your mouth.

Our speech was given to us by God for creative purposes. The entire universe was formed with words. God spoke everything into existence. On the first day of creation, God said, "I command light to shine!" And light started shining. Then, on the second day He said, "I command a dome to separate the water above it from the water below it." God made the dome and named it "Sky." Each day He created something new with His words. Until finally, He created us.

We were made in His image. And therefore we were created with that same power to use words as a creative force in the earth. I know this is a bold statement, but I believe the life you are living right now reflects what you have been saying.

Words are a piece of our spirit expressed in sound. That is why people often say, "it is not what you said but how you said it." They hear what I like to call the person's "come from." Your "come from" is the force or spirit behind what you say. The words we speak are always filtered through the posture of our hearts. And that filtering process often determines how our words land in the ears and on the heart of others.

Your words don't find their meaning as they leave your mouth, they are conceived in your heart first. The Bible says that a good man brings good things out of the good stored up in his heart, and an evil man brings evil things out of the evil stored up in his heart (Luke 6:45). That is why it is so important for us to develop intimacy in our relationships with God. When you spend your life hiding your heart from God, He never gets the chance to clean it out. And overtime it becomes messy and this eventually is reflected in your comments and conversations with others.

This concept is illustrated clearly in Matthew chapter 12, verses 36 and 37: "You have minds like a snake pit! How do you suppose what you say is worth anything when you are so foul-minded? It's your heart, not the dictionary, that gives meaning to your words. A good person produces good deeds and words season after season. An evil person is a blight on the orchard. Let me tell you something: Every one of these careless words is going to come back to haunt you. There will be a time of reckoning. Words are powerful; take them seriously. Words can be your salvation. Words can also be your damnation."

This passage of scripture shows us clearly how seriously God takes the words we speak. We should take them seriously too.

Ezekiel chapter 36, verse 26 explains that when you start to walk with God, He will give you *"a new heart...and a new spirit will [He] put within you: and [He] will take away the stony heart out of your flesh, and [He] will give you a heart of flesh.*

Because of this truth, we have access to a heart with Christ at the center. The question is, will you speak out of your new heart or neglect it and try to continue speaking out of your old stony heart?

I love the way this idea is explained in James chapter 3, verses 5 to 10. Let's read it:

Words have Power to Curse or to Bless.

James 3:5-10 (MSG) reads "a bit in the mouth of a horse controls the whole horse." A small rudder on a huge ship in the hands of a skilled captain sets a course in the face of the strongest winds. A word out of your mouth may seem of no account, but it can accomplish nearly anything—or destroy it! It only takes a spark, remember, to set off a forest fire. A careless or wrongly placed word out of your mouth can do that. By our speech we can ruin the world, turn harmony to chaos, throw mud on a reputation, send the whole world up in smoke and go up in smoke with it, smoke right from the pit of hell. This is scary: You can tame a tiger, but you can't tame a tongue—it's never been done. The tongue runs wild, a wanton killer. With our tongue, we bless God our Father; with the same tongue, we curse the very men and women he made in his image. Curses and blessings out of the same mouth!

Do you see why I love the message version of these scriptures? It's on point! It clearly depicts the power and potential of our speech.

The Bible is full of verses about the power of our words. And in order to fully understand it you need to study the subject diligently.

Let's slow down for a minute and read a few other scriptures about "the power of the tongue" and the power of words:

Words Have The Power of Life And Death

"Death and life are in the power of the tongue, and those who love

it will eat its fruits" (Proverbs 18:21).

Words Reveal What's in Our Hearts

"Either make the tree good and its fruit good, or make the tree bad and its fruit bad, for the tree is known by its fruit. You brood of vipers! How can you speak good, when you are evil? For out of the abundance of the heart the mouth speaks. The good person out of his good treasure brings forth good, and the evil person out of his evil treasure brings forth evil" (Matthew 12:33-35).

Words Give Grace

"Let no corrupting talk come out of your mouths, but only such as is good for building up, as fits the occasion, that it may give grace to those who hear" (Ephesians 4:29).

Words Can Be Weapons & Words Can Heal

"There is one whose rash words are like sword thrusts, but the tongue of the wise brings healing" (Proverbs 12:18).

Words Maintain Our Life & Words Breakdown Our Life

"Whoever guards his mouth preserves his life; he who opens wide his lips comes to ruin" (Proverbs 13:3).

Our words are crucial to the success of our lives. Just as we read, God has given us the power to speak life or death into our circumstances. To bless or to curse. To build or to break. Many times, we can avoid a lot of challenges we have in life by simply controlling our tongue.

Scripture even says that if we can control what comes out of our mouths, we can control ourselves in every other way. God is letting us know that many of our self-control issues and our habits that could potentially spin our lives off course (overeating, overspending, lying, and/or gossiping) start with what is coming out our mouths.

The Bible also says in Proverbs chapter 21, verse 23 that a person who can keep their mouth under control can also keep their soul from many troubles. This can be tough because on a daily bases we are surrounded by people who probably aren't practicing these same principles. So, the temptation to be careless with your speech will always be there.

Trust me. I know about it.

This is one of the areas that I consistently work on in my life. I like to talk. God made me that way. He gave me the gift of communication, but if this gift is misused or poorly managed it will become problematic. And the same is true for you.

God wants us to be His examples on the Earth. One of the surest signs that we are His disciples and that we understand how to love people is the way we direct and manage our conversations. This includes what we talk about publicly and privately. It even includes how we speak to people when we are upset. All of it matters!

I had a Christian client a few years ago that was struggling with maintaining her integrity. Her ability to keep her word was delaying her destiny. Lying under pressure was a defense mechanism she had mastered over the years as a way of not having to be accountable for her actions.

After weeks of uncovering this issue we realized that at the root of her character flaw there were a few words planted in her mind by her mother when she was a child. Her mother would say things like, "please answer the phone and tell them I'm not here." She would reinforce her request by explaining to my client that it was just a "white lie." The only problem was that there were many white lies and "gray" areas being demonstrated in her home. Many of these lies were more severe than simply lying about being home.

On the surface, I know it doesn't seem like a big deal, but that tiny seed grew in my client. She began repeating the same kind of behavior she had seen as a child. "White Lies" became acceptable and they eventually grew into all types of behaviors that compromised her integrity in her relationships and in her business. For example, lying about her electricity being out to excuse her missed report deadline. Or saying she was in traffic to avoid addressing her constant tardiness.

Over time, this "White Lie" behavior spread and developed into a way of life. She stopped resisting it and accepted it as a part of her identity. She would make excuses to avoid confrontation and make statements that reinforced this false identity. Lying to stay comfortable became her way of survival. She would say things like, "this is just who I am, I am just bad at managing time or being organized."

Clearly it was not her mom's intention to plant a seed in her daughter's heart that would produce such a harvest. But because of the power of words, unfortunately that "White Lie" seed took root. That is exactly what words are designed to do. They are designed to be planted and bear fruit. But the type of fruit they produce, will always depend on the seed that was planted.

Think about your life for a moment. Are you purposefully using your words to build or break your friends? Your family? Your health? Your finances? Your future?

Words are how we manage and navigate our lives. On any given day, we are either talking or hearing people talk for hours at a time. Speech becomes the scaffolding that props up every relationship we have. It's important that we use wisdom and apply what the Word of God is teaching us about managing our mouths.

Often, in our Christian walk, we experience trials and tribulations. After all, living a life for Christ is not as easy as you would think. I mean we do have an entire book full of instructions, that we just need to follow. But it's not as simple as just following the rules. Deeply understanding Biblical Truths and applying those principles is a whole different story.

The Bible does warn us about the storms in life. In John chapter 16, verse 33, the Bible says; *"In this world you will have trouble. But take heart! I have overcome the world."*

When we read this scripture, it sounds great. We are overcomers in Christ! But what happens when you get into an argument with someone you love, or a co-worker responds to you in a way that should be censured around children. It can all make you want to leave your love-walk and Bible-talk at home.

In my life, there have been many times when I have failed miserably at managing my mouth. And there will be times where you miss the mark too, but God's grace is sufficient to help you change, but there has to be a true desire in you to change in order to ignite the transformation.

Talking To People

How we talk to people often reflects how we talk to ourselves. It's important that we represent the Love of Christ when we are talking to people. In order to do this, we need to love ourselves with the Love of Christ as well. If you are harsh and judgmental with yourself, you will communicate that same type of talk with others. If you receive grace and forgiveness for yourself, you will more easily share grace and forgiveness with others.

The Bible tells us in John chapter 13, verse 35, that people will know that we are His disciples because of the way we love each other. Not because of what we have achieved, or for the material possessions we've acquired. It will be our love for one another that transforms our lives, our communities and our world.

How do we demonstrate that love?

We undoubtedly show love through our actions. But outside our actions, it's our words that demonstrate to people our love and level of maturity in Christ. This is especially revealed when we are under pressure.

I have noticed in my life that the more intentional I am about what I say, the more smoothly everything flows. My career, relationships, finances all tend to thrive when I consciously manage my mouth. Doing this takes practice, but it is worth it! And over time, you will become a much more effective communicator and you will see harvest in every area of your life.

Now, of course when we are getting along with people perfectly well it is easier to say the right things at the right times. But what happens when people push your buttons and you feel like giving them a piece of your mind?

You could surrender to being petty and tell them everything you think is wrong with them. You could fire off a round of insults or be passive aggressive and mumble a few sarcastic comments from across the room. Whatever your reactionary impulse is, if it doesn't reflect God's love, then there is some internal work that needs to be done in your spirit and soul. When you make sure your spirit is saturated with the Word of God you can learn how to respond better each time.

Think about how God talks to us in His word, or when He speaks to you directly. Even when He is correcting us, there is always an undertone that affirms His love and purposes for our life. He always communicates in a way that reminds us that He is for us and not against us.

Imagine how your relationships would flourish if people knew 100% of the time that you loved them unconditionally.

I bet we would see people show up differently in our classrooms, in our churches, in our businesses and in our lives. When you grant unconditional love, it frees people up from trying to be perfect. It allows them to be present in the relationship without fearing your rejection. This environment creates the opportunity for a closer connection. It creates trust and new levels of vulnerability. Now, I am not saying that every person you meet needs to be your "bestie", but I am saying that every encounter you have with another individual, should be intentional. People should leave your presence knowing they are seen, heard, and loved.

I often think about the Bible and Jesus's life. I think about how He moved from town to town, encountering huge crowds of people. He was on a serious assignment to come to Earth, live blamelessly, and then die for us all. That could have been His only focus. But even under that extreme level of pressure, even on the days when He might have been exhausted or overwhelmed, He would always leave people knowing they were loved and accepted.

There is not one single encounter where Jesus didn't leave people in a better condition than He found them in. Isn't that amazing? I know we are not Jesus, but we are made in God's image, and we have been gifted with the Holy Spirit. Therefore, we have been given a supernatural capacity to love people. In the times where we feel like it is impossible, and people have hurt us deeply, God has promised us that His grace is sufficient and that His power is made perfect in our weaknesses. With his help, we can respond from a place of love even in the most uncomfortable and painful situations.

Talking to people and making them feel love requires much more energy than simply going through the motions. Being fake with people doesn't require much energy. But being real with others takes some work. For this reason, Jesus would retreat and pray before engaging with the masses. Praying gave Him access to that supernatural power for loving people. If Jesus needed that, how much more do we need it?

When you feel pressured to give into your emotions during your conversations, follow Jesus's example and pray! It's our connection with God, that gives us access to unlimited love as we communicate and relate to others. And the more we learn to receive His love, the better we can love other people.

Through Christ, we can respond above our anger and other emotions. We have access to wisdom on how to react and respond that we can tap into when we are upset. Human nature would have us respond to personal attacks and arguments in anger, bitterness, and with harsh words but through Jesus Christ we have been delivered from these less than higher principles. Through the resurrection of Jesus we have been freed from sin. This includes being free from angry and irresponsible emotional responses. What Jesus did on the cross not only took us from death to life, but gave us access to a new heart and a new mind.

Acting out of fearful and angry emotions, does not match the fruits of the Holy Spirit (Galatians 5:22). We are called to respond to people with love, joy, peace, patience, kindness, goodness, and self-control. This kind of response is required of all of us because our Christian life is about living out the image of Christ. We are being transformed into His image daily, and therefore we should strive to live as He lived.

Jesus was persecuted and falsely accused of all kinds of offenses, but He still operated from a place of love. He even prayed for the forgiveness of those attacking Him. In Luke chapter 6, verse 28, the Bible tells us to bless those who curse us and pray for those who mistreat us.

Jesus is both a lion and a lamb, and so are we. But He had the wisdom to understand how these seemingly contradictory identities interact. Many times, when Jesus was attacked, He would take on the posture of a lamb instead of attacking back like a lion. Choosing to humble yourself and respond as a lamb and not as a lion when you are being tested is pleasing to God. It shows we are willing to put Him and other people above our desires. I know it might feel like the weak way to respond when you are being treated unfairly. It actually requires much more strength to do so. Reacting wisely as a lamb didn't make Jesus any less powerful. In fact, Jesus's biggest upset to worldly standards was submitting to the cross and dying like a lamb instead of roaring like a lion and climbing down from His death. This choice wasn't made from a place of weakness. It might not have been what the people were expecting but the lamb was what they needed, not the lion.

Scripture says in Proverbs chapter 15, verse 1 that a *"gentle answer turns away wrath, but a harsh word stirs up anger."* This truth determines the health of every single relationship in your life.

Every relationship, whether personal or professional has an account, just like the one you would open at a bank. Our words function as deposits or withdrawals to those accounts. Who wants to go to the bank and find out that their account is empty, or even worse, that it's in the negative! Nobody! But this is what happens to many of us in our relationships when we don't sow enough positive words into the hearts of the people that we love and that God has entrusted us with. We must consistently work to build and maintain a positive balance. In the same way that you make deposits into your bank account, when you want to see it multiply and grow.

When we deposit negative words into our relationship accounts, we subtract from the health of that relationship. But on the same hand if you say nothing, the account will always be empty. Be smart about how you make deposits and withdrawals in your relationships with your words.

Ask yourself, how do people feel after they speak to me? Are they Insulted or inspired? Built up or broken down?

The main thing is to ultimately make sure that your communication with others is pleasing to God. I am not suggesting that you should overthink every interaction you have, but you should definitely give your words some thought before you let them leave your mouth. You are responsible for your words and your tone, but you are not necessarily responsible for the filter that people process them with. Sometimes, unfortunately, even when you yield to what God wants you to say and how He wants you to say it, people will still misinterpret you. But that doesn't mean we shouldn't try.

The way I approach this is by asking myself, "Do I have peace about what I said and how I said it? Was what I said pleasing to God?" If I can undoubtedly respond with a yes, then I know I did my best. If not, I know that I need to seek God, revisit my response, and form it to match His desires for my communication with that person.

My relationship with my mother is a perfect example of this communicative process. I had to learn how to intentionally check the posture of my heart when speaking to her. This is one of many relationships in my life where I have seen the power of sowing positive words work.

My mom and I have had some very challenging times over the years. We were very close when I was younger, but as I grew up, things changed. We stopped seeing eye to eye. It got so bad I almost gave up on the relationship. I got very close to surrendering to the dysfunction it presented. But as I matured in Christ, I realized how much she meant to me and how much I wanted our relationship to work. So, I decided to work on it. This was not an easy decision to make because I knew deep down that if I asked God to work on my relationship with my mother, that He was going to start by working on me first! I decided to be more committed to the future of our relationship then I was to our past. I wanted to love her better. Even still, there was a part of me that was unsure if I would be able to do this. I was afraid that if I did everything necessary to love my mother better still the love would not be reciprocated. But God continued to work with me in this area. I guess you could say He softened my heart and strengthened my faith at the same time.

In my prayer time, I could feel Him increasing my capacity to receive His love and as a result I had more love to give to others, including my mother. I started to see my mom as God sees her. The more I engaged in God's view of my mother, the more I wanted to love her. As my heart changed I realized she was just like me. She just wanted to be loved unconditionally.

The process was not perfect. There were things that threatened to rise from our past and destroyed our precariously healing relationship. I would remember mistakes she had made but the truth was, I had already forgiven her and I was committed to loving her. I just needed to walk it out in my actions and with my words.

One day I made the decision to only sow words and actions of love. I never told this to anyone, I simply kept it between God and me. I remember saying and doing things that were completely out of my comfort zone. I made some sacrifices and every once in a while I took some sucker punches. The kind of punches the devil throws to try and make you regret that you ever decided to trust God.

But after some time, I started to notice some changes. I could see my mom's heart opening more towards me. It seemed like my words of love created a safe place for her to show up without fear of being judged or wronged. She could sense I could now see what was good about her.

She started sending me encouraging messages and even cards in the mail. In my mind I thought, "Maybe my mom has always treated me like this, but I couldn't see it." Either way, I knew it felt different and that God was restoring our relationship. We started hanging out more. In a way, you could say we became friends. We started making plans to see each other more often and on a more consistent basis. I knew this is what God wanted. Even now, I still see the results of the positive words I sewed into my mother's heart, both privately and publicly. And I am thankful that God gave me the courage to love her better and make positive deposits in our relationship account.

This is what I did with my mother, but this is how we should love everybody.

I encourage you to reflect on the relationships in your life and the words you are depositing or withdrawing from them. I challenge you to intentionally improve the way you speak to those around you. You would be amazed at how managing your mouth and using your words for good can transform your life and the lives of those around you. Don't take this subject lightly. Your words are powerful and they matter!

Talking About People

Let's keep it 100! We all know that gossiping is wrong, and we shouldn't do it. Of course, that doesn't mean we will not be tempted to do so. How do we learn to honor God and people in our conversations, both publicly and privately?

When I started studying the subject of gossip, I noticed that a lot of the scriptures were in the book of proverbs, which is a consider to be "the book of wisdom." That alone points us to the fact that gossiping is not wise. When people gossip, they are lacking one of two things, wisdom or self-control.

Wisdom is the application of what you know and understand. When you operate with wisdom, you understand the consequences of gossip, and as a result you refrain from it. But truth be told, God knows we will be tempted to say bad things about people, and that bad things will be said about us. But He wants us to move away from this behavior and into a wise and honoring speech.

If you have this knowledge and wisdom, but you still choose to gossip about others, it could be an issue of self-control.

Bottom line, gossiping is not ok! This is something we all know already, and we are going to approach it directly. No sugar coating allowed. Let's go to the Bible and see what God says about this.

James chapter 1, verse 26 says *"those who consider themselves religious and yet do not keep a tight rein on their tongues deceive themselves, and their religion is worthless."* When I read this scripture, I thought to myself, "Yikes! Worthless? This is serious!" To that God responded, "Yes, it is!"

This scripture sets the tone for everything we need to understand about gossip. When we badmouth other people, we are hurting others and deceiving ourselves. When we gossip, we think we are exposing someone else, but we are revealing the quality of our own character.

Let's make something clear, there is a form of malicious gossip, where you are intentionally trying to put someone else down. But there are also times when we allow ourselves to share information about others that we were told in confidence, and in doing so we break people's trust.

I heard a pastor once say, "if you are not a character in the story, it is not your story to tell." And that is what we need to keep in mind when we are communicating with other people. And although, we may feel like it's not a big deal, this is still a form of gossip.

Managing our mouth is not only about what we say to ourselves, it is also about how we talk to and about others. Words are seeds, as quickly as you are talking about someone else, you are planting the garden of your own life. Proverbs chapter 18, verses 6 and 7 says, *"The lips of fools bring them strife, and their mouths invite a beating. The mouths of fools are their undoing, and their lips are a snare to their very lives."* When you're talking about somebody else, you're eating that seed, they are not. The words are coming from out of your heart and out of your mouth.

Let's look at a few other scriptures:

"Brothers and sisters, do not slander one another. Anyone who speaks against a brother or sister or judges them speaks against the law and judges it. When you judge the law, you are not keeping it, but sitting in judgment on it" (James 4:11).

"Do not go about spreading slander among your people. Do not do anything that endangers your neighbor's life. I am the LORD" (Leviticus 19:16).

"A gossip betrays a confidence, but a trustworthy person keeps a secret" (Proverbs 11:13).

"A perverse person stirs up conflict, and a gossip separates close friends" (Proverbs 16:28).

"A gossip betrays a confidence; so, avoid anyone who talks too much" (Proverbs 20:19).

These are only a few examples, but there are so many others that make it clear not only that gossiping is bad, but that it can bring severe consequences into our lives and the lives of others. It can destroy marriages, ministries, businesses and friendships.

If after understanding all of this, we still choose to badmouth people, we are simply being foolish. The Bible says in Proverbs chapter 10, verse 18, "whoever conceals hatred with lying lips and spreads slander is a fool." And I don't know about you, but I don't want to go through my life being a fool because I couldn't manage my mouth.

The good news is the Bible also advises us on how to fight against this. The first thing we need to do is to spend time with God and pray for wisdom about managing our mouths. Then we need to exercise that wisdom and practice being intentional about thinking before we speak. Psalm chapter 141, verse 3 says *"set a guard over my mouth, LORD; keep watch over the door of my lips."*

And in Proverbs chapter 17, verse 9 it says, *"Whoever would foster love covers over an offense, but whoever repeats the matter separates close friends."* This means that we need to cultivate and nurture our level of love for people, so that when they disappoint us or hurt us, we don't slander them. When we've built up deep love for people, even when they hurt us we can cover them with love, like Christ covers us.

It all starts with us reading the Word of God, and then spending time with God so that we can be transformed into

His image. Then we can see people the way God sees them and love them in the way He does. I wish I could tell you that there is a shortcut to living your best life and unlocking your God-given potential, but there isn't. You must show up, tell the truth, and do the work.

Speaking In Agreement With The Word

Managing your mouth also means monitoring your mouth and making sure what comes out of it lines up with the Word of God. The more you know your Bible, the easier this will become.

I'm not talking about saying Hallelujah and Amen every time someone asks you how you are doing or says, "Good morning." But our words do need to come into alignment with scripture. For example, you can't constantly be saying you're not enough, when God's word says that "you are fearfully and wonderfully made" (Psalm 139:14) Or confessing that you're always sick, when the word says that "But he was pierced for our transgressions, he was crushed for our iniquities; the punishment that brought us peace was on him, and by his wounds we are healed" (Isaiah 53:5).

Now understand this, people can get caught up in religious culture and begin mindlessly quoting the word of God all the time. Adding Biblical jargon to every salutation doesn't make you closer to God. People can say things like, "I am blessed and highly favored" but nothing about their life reflects that statement. Remember, in your relationship with God, it's not about always saying and doing the right things. It's about having the right heart.

Managing your mouth to agree with God's Word means you are willing to course correct when you recognize that what you are saying is incongruent with scripture. Pray and allow the Holy Spirit to reveal the areas of your conversations that need some attention. This includes self-talk! Commit to agreeing with God's Word and consistently adjust your speech accordingly. And when you don't know what to say, just be quiet or speak the Word only!

Silence is Golden

Many times, silence is the best option for handling a stressful situation. I am not saying we should ignore people when they challenge, persecute, or irritate us. However, I am suggesting that you should not react out of your initial emotions or offense.

I had a mentor who helped me a lot in this area. As I've mentioned, responding to people in love and saying the right things under pressure was extremely difficult for me. I believed that when people did things that made me feel disappointed or hurt, whether they did it intentionally or unintentionally, that they needed to be called out on it.

My mentor and I worked together on strategies that would help me to respond better when I felt emotionally triggered by tough business situations or the actions of people.

She taught me how to create "measured responses." Essentially these were responses that were thought of ahead of time. When a situation arose where I felt uncomfortable and would normally lash out, I now had prepared responses ready to use.

Some of those responses were, "I hear what you are saying. I didn't know you felt that way. I don't want to say anything that would damage our relationship. It would be great if you would allow me to take some time and think about the best way to respond. Is it ok if I get back to you later today or tomorrow?"

This is just one of many "measured responses" my mentor and I created together. At first, I felt it was cheesy and unauthentic. However, after implementing them, I realized they were quite effective for several reasons. Using the "measured responses" created space and gave me time to be quiet. And in that silence the Holy Spirit would begin to work in my heart and my emotions and give me the right words to say. I noticed a huge difference in the outcomes of problematic situations when I responded by using these "measured responses." As I continued to grow and practice responding in love under pressure that muscle in my spiritual self-continued to strengthen.

As I was writing this chapter, I had yet another opportunity to practice what I am preaching. God is good that way, He always puts us in situations that illustrate His truth, if we are willing to listen.

I was on the phone working with my Creative Content Editor online and right at a crucial part of our meeting, she interrupted with something that was completely off topic. I immediately became irritated, because she did this often. As a result, we would get distracted, lose track of time and our meeting would totally go off course. As I was trying to get us back on track, she kept fighting to be heard with her off-topic conversation. I could feel the situation quickly escalating. I was focused on meeting the deadline! So, out of my frustration, I hung up the call. I realized in that moment, that using one of my "measured responses" instead of hanging up, would have been a better option.

But even still, hanging up the call gave me some time to reflect and think about how I wanted to respond. I was of course tempted to text her several times, while I was still in my feelings. But the Holy Spirit kept prompting me to be still and quiet. As I yielded to the silence, I began to hear clearly from God what I should say next. His voice guided me into the right timing and the right words to write back to my editor. I also apologized for hanging up.

Once I texted her, she expressed her gratitude for the loving way I had responded. She also accepted my apology. The next day she even mentioned that she had notice that my response was filtered through God's love.

The silence was beneficial. Being quiet when we are under attack can be just as powerful as making our point in a conversation. In Psalm chapter 46, verses 10 the Bible says, *"be still and know that I am God."* That is what being silent is all about. It allows God to reveal His truth in situations and it creates space for us to receive his direction.

There are many other scriptures that talk about the benefits of silence. Let's read some:

"A time to tear and a time to mend, a time to be silent and a time to speak" (Ecclesiastes 3:7).

"Even fools are thought wise if they keep silent, and discerning if they hold their tongues" (Proverbs 17:28).

"He who guards his mouth and his tongue, guards his soul from troubles" (Proverbs 21:23).

"He who restrains his words has knowledge, and he who has a cool spirit is a man of understanding" (Proverbs 17:27).

If you are not practicing this in the way you respond under pressure, I encourage you to take some time and create your own "measured responses" as a buffer to create time for you to be silent and access wisdom. This will not only save you a lot of trouble, but it will also be pleasing to God. And when you act in agreement with God's Word, you always win!

Speak Beyond Your Emotions

Learning how to live and speak beyond your emotions is critical for your spiritual and personal growth. If you don't learn how to communicate beyond your emotions you will never mature to your full capacity, personally or professionally. It is not enough to be super gifted or an intellectual giant, but still be bound by your emotions. Our feelings change, and they change quickly. One day you may feel like quitting your job and the next day you may feel like running the company. Emotions are fickle, and you cannot put your trust in them. If you do, they will lead you astray. God designed us to live by faith not our emotions. Living and operating by faith gives us access to spiritual dimensions and power that can only function when we live by higher principles. Living and operating from our emotions leaves us raw and unstable.

The Bible reads, "If you walk in the spirit, you will not fulfill the desires of the flesh" (Galatians 5:16). When we rise above our emotions and choose to respond with words that are rooted and grounded in our love for God we can fruitfully overcome any situation.

Now, I'm not saying you shouldn't feel or have emotions. God gave us emotions for a reason. For example, anger is designed to help us set boundaries. Joy is a signal for us to celebrate. Our emotions were given to us to help us grow. There are many examples in the Bible where Jesus verbally expresses emotions.

One of those examples is the story about Jesus and Lazarus in John chapter 11, verses 1 to 44.

Jesus was very close to Lazarus, Mary, and Martha. He would visit them often and have dinner at their home. Lazarus got sick, so his sisters sent a messenger to inform Jesus that the one He loved was sick. They expected Him to show up and save the day.

When Jesus heard this, He said, "This sickness will not end in death. No, it is for God's glory so that God's Son may be glorified through it." Jesus loved all three of them, yet He stayed where he was for two more days, delaying an arrival that was deeply expected. Then He said to His disciples, "Let us go back to Judea."

During those two days of waiting, Lazarus died. I can't even imagine how the sisters may have felt. Jesus had not shown up on time. Can you imagine that? Have you ever felt as if God showed up late in a situation in your life?

Nevertheless, what happened after that is one of the most amazing parts of the Bible. Jesus resurrected Lazarus from the dead!

Yet what happened in verses 21 to 37, has always caught my attention. Let's read through the story together:

21 "Lord," Martha said to Jesus, "if you had been here, my brother would not have died. 22 But I know that even now God will give you whatever you ask."
23 Jesus said to her, "Your brother will rise again."
24 Martha answered, "I know he will rise again in the resurrection at the last day."
25 Jesus said to her, "I am the resurrection and the life. The one who believes in me will live, even though they die; 26 and whoever lives by believing in me will never die. Do you believe this?"
27 "Yes, Lord," she replied, "I believe that you are the Messiah, the Son of God, who is to come into the world."
28 After she had said this, she went back and called her sister Mary aside. "The Teacher is here," she said, "and is asking for you." 29 When Mary heard this, she got up quickly and went to him. 30 Now Jesus had not yet entered the village, but was still at the place where Martha had met him. 31 When the Jews who had been with Mary in the house, comforting her, noticed how quickly

*she got up and went out, they followed her, supposing she was
going to the tomb to mourn there.*
*32 When Mary reached the place where Jesus was and saw him,
she fell at his feet and said, "Lord, if you had been here, my
brother would not have died."*
*33 When Jesus saw her weeping, and the Jews who had come
along with her also weeping, he was deeply moved in spirit and
troubled. 34 "Where have you laid him?" he asked.*
"Come and see, Lord," they replied.
35 Jesus wept.
36 Then the Jews said, "See how he loved him!"
*37 But some of them said, "Could not he who opened the eyes of
the blind man have kept this man from dying?"*

Even in those times where we see no hope, God is never
late. No matter what situation you are facing, God is always
with you!

In these verses, we can see people talking to and about
Jesus. They questioned, doubted, and accused Him. People
were "disappointed" by the fact that He had not arrived
sooner. But He didn't react emotionally to their
disappointment. He responded to them with comfort and from
a place of love.

Jesus could have copped an attitude. He could have
allowed himself to be triggered by their emotions of unbelief
and reacted by saying something harsh like, "People! Stop
crying! Don't you know I am the resurrection? Get your lives
together!"

I mean, Jesus had even previously explained to Mary that He
had the power to resurrect Lazarus, but the situation had
escalated so much, she couldn't understand Him. She was
saddened by how the conversation unfolded. She knew Jesus
could have done something to heal Lazarus before he died,
but now she felt abandoned.

Nevertheless, Jesus continued to respond to her in love and showed all the mourners compassion.

He saw people grieving, and was deeply moved in spirit. He understood that beyond their tears for the loss of a loved one, they were also experiencing pain because of they lost hope in the situation. Jesus saw this and felt sadness for three reasons. First, He felt compassion for their suffering. Secondly, He felt sad about their lack of faith. And finally, He knew that at the bottom of it all, Lazarus's death was nothing more than the consequences of sin on Earth. This is what He had come for! To defeat death, not only for Lazarus, but for all who believed in Him! So, Jesus showed great emotion. Jesus wept!

Emotions are not bad. It is how we react and respond to them that matters. Jesus's love for Lazarus was questioned and His power was doubted but, yet He rose beyond the situation and loved on those around Him.

There are so many other moments in the Bible where Jesus shows us how to speak above our emotions. He exercised self-control when tempted by the devil in the wilderness. Time after time the enemy tried to get Him to respond in anger or pride, but He resisted the devil by responding with the Word of God (Luke 4:1-13). He patiently asked His disciples to support Him in prayer right before He was arrested to be crucified. The first time He asked, they fell asleep! Still, the second time, He asked nicely (Luke 22: 40, 46). One time, Jesus was alerted about a woman caught in adultery, He reacted first by addressing her accusers. "Let any one of you who is without sin be the first to throw a stone at her" he said. And He addressed the woman by dismissing their judgements against her and encouraging her to move away from her sinful life (John 8:1-11).

Emotions can make us feel crazy, but God has given us the authority to manage them. So, we are to lead and not to follow, when it comes to operating beyond our emotions.

Josh Squires, a Pastor in Columbia, South Carolina, explained this very clearly in his article "Two Blind Guides, Conforming Our Mind and Heart to God's." He said, "Don't follow your heart; our hearts were not made to be followed, but to be led."

Remember the story about my editor? As you know, there are always two sides to every story. Listening to her version, I realized that there was a lesson in managing our mouths, that we could all learn from her as well. I didn't want you to miss out on receiving that valuable insight. So, for the sake of keeping it "real", I asked my editor if she would be willing to share her version of the story. Thankfully, she agreed.

This is what she said:

When Ashley hung up on me, my first instinct was to respond to her in a very emotional and impulsive way. I wanted to bombard her with text messages expressing my original point and my frustration. In my heart, I knew that would only make things worse.

Ashley is someone I work with, but she is also my entrusted coach. Most importantly, she is my dear friend. Working with someone in such a variety of ways can make things complicated but it can also make things special. During my coaching sessions with Ashley, we had been working on improving how I manage my emotions when I fear rejection and addressing my overall fear of man. When Ashley hung up on me, I felt my old reactions rising.

Normally, I would keep fighting to be heard. I would have sent her a series of overwhelming text messages. But this time when I got triggered, I was more conscious, which allowed me to be intentional about speaking above my emotions. I was able to regain my power, recognizing that I could make a choice about how I wanted to respond. I did not want to be a victim of my emotions.

So, like Ashley, I also decided to stay silent and gave God time to work in both of our hearts. I had to humble myself and trust that God would communicate what I was feeling to her. I decided to yield to God's voice and apply what I had been learning with Ashley. This required humility and patience. Again, this was the opposite of what I would normally do.

There was so much I still wanted to say. I mean, no matter how annoying I was being, I thought hanging up was rude. But then I asked myself, what is more important right now, making my point, or pleasing God with my words and taking care of my relationship with Ashley? Clearly the second option was a better one. So, I decide to trust God and be silent.

When she finally responded, I laughed and felt so happy. I knew within seeing her first message come through, that God's love was at the center. I was silent, and God came through! He is faithful.

I replied to Ashley and accepted her apology, I also apologized for interrupting our meeting. I was still a little caught up in my emotions. Therefore, I decided to give the situation more time, so I could speak above my emotions. I explained this to Ashley and she replied, "Amen!"

Ashley and I were scheduled to meet for business again the next day. And so, we did. Before the meeting started Ashley suggested that we open our hearts and clear the air from the day before. She asked me if I had anything that I wanted to share. In my head, I was thinking, "Of course!" But I was still practicing the principles of rising above my fears and emotions. So, I took a moment and expressed myself in a way that was clear and in agreement with the Holy Spirit. I could sense my choice of words was effective. Ashley understood me completely and we moved forward freely.

I don't know what you think, but in a situation like this, many people would have reacted differently, and it could have even ended the writing project all together. I am thankful that it didn't. For me this was confrontational success. We had gone through a rough situation and had risen above it with God's help.

During the silent moment, we both sought for God's guidance in our own way and listened for how to respond. This made all the difference in the world. We both responded in a loving way and it allowed us the privilege of resolving the issue with wisdom and peace. There is so much power in learning to be silent and still. It gives God access to our hearts.

That is her side of the story and as you can see, we both learned a lot about the essence of this chapter. God can use you to help people develop and be developing you at the exact same time. Isn't that wonderful?

As you can see from my experience with my editor, it is so important not to let our emotions dictate every word that comes out of our mouths. And although we could have both done better from the start, her not pushing her point, me not hanging up the phone, God's grace was sufficient. It made up for our weaknesses and at the same time helped us both grow. It revealed the pathway for us to reconcile. It takes practice and patience with ourselves and others, when it comes to managing our mouths. At times, it can be challenging but it is not impossible. If you manage this area of your life now, you can avoid regretting it later.

CHAPTER 7

DISCIPLE = DISCIPLINE

Adisciple is a follower or a learner. It is someone who takes on the teachings of another person. Since we are Disciples of Christ, we should conform our ways, to the ways of Jesus. The more we follow Him and obey Him, the more we are transformed into His image and ultimately our true identity.

Have you ever heard this saying, *"the best leaders are followers."*? This defines those who exhibit high-level leadership qualities because they tend to be very good at listening and following directions. Yes, I know it sounds simple, but this an under developed competency in many. You might be thinking to yourself, How difficult can following directions be? But have you ever given someone instructions and they didn't follow them? Maybe you have even been that person once or twice. In our walk with God, following directions is the only way to ensure our growth and prosperity. Anytime we decide to take a short cut, we arrest our development and risk losing everything.

In my professional life, I have worked with several organizations and corporations, helping them to improve their employee's performance. I conducted workshops, facilitated team building exercises and creative activities to help their employees develop their character and enhance communication skills.

When doing these presentations, I often noticed that it didn't matter what company, the demographics of the employees, or the environment, the main thing people struggled with was *"following directions."* I would give very specific and succinct instructions and the employees would still neglect the instructions all together or manipulate them to create their own version of what I asked them to do.

This puzzled me. I understand that people don't follow directions for a multitude of reasons. In some cases, the instructions may not be clear and in other cases people enjoy figuring things out for themselves better. But I realized after digging deeper with my clients that a lot of times, this happened because people think that they know better. They think that their way of doing things is most efficient or "right". And I noticed that when these teams in my workshops took on this type of mindset, they would end up following their own agenda and it would eventually lead to their groups breaking down out of frustration. While working, they could see the shift in the morale taking place within their group, but nevertheless, they would still continue going in their own direction.

I saw how the tasks or assignments I gave them would take much longer, and as a result their outcomes were usually mediocre or average. In some cases, the teams of employees would give up and not even finish the assignment. At the end of each workshop, I would take time to debrief with the different groups and they would always conclude that although there were many reasons why they didn't reach their expected outcome, eventually they would conclude that their problem was their unwillingness *to follow directions*. As for the people who did follow the instructions that were given, they did not run into much frustration, they were able to move faster working together, things ran more smoothly and their outcomes exceeded expectations.

I think many times this happens to us when we are learning to follow and trust God. We allow ourselves to get influenced by the ideas of others or get distracted by our own motives and we decide to go in our own direction. We do things our own way and it only sets us back. It delays our spiritual, personal, and professional growth and ends up leaving us with average results. Instead of following God's instructions from the beginning and allowing Him to be the final authority in our lives.

It is imperative that we DO what the Word of God says without filtering it through our own motives and meanings. We must be willing to take God at His Word if we want to unlock our full potential and live our best lives.

Following Christ requires discipline.

The good thing about God's discipline though, is that we can always be certain it's coming from a place of love.

Proverbs chapter 3, verse 12, says in The Message version, *"It's the child he loves that God corrects; a father's delight is behind all this."*

God disciplines us *because* He loves us. He delights in us as His sons and daughters. He does this to help us grow, to mature in faith, to increase our strength and ultimately to transform us into His image. He wants the very best for us, and that requires discipline.

The Bible says in John chapter 8, verse 32, "If you live by what I say, you are truly my disciples." Notice that it doesn't say if you *read*, or if you *take note of*, or if you *speak ab*out what [He] says. It clearly says, if you live by God's Words then you are His disciples. In another version, this part is translated as *abide in*, which means to "comply with, obey, observe, follow, keep to, hold to, conform to, adhere to, stick to, stand by, act in accordance with".

If we want to see the Word of God fulfilled in our lives, we need to live it! Not just one time, but *consistently*. Therefore, learning to follow instructions is so important.

Now, let's be honest. Living this thing out is not easy. Discipline is a skill that must be developed. And once you learn it, it has to be practiced. Practice makes permanent. The reason I say permanent and not perfect is because we are not perfect, that is why we need God. Practicing starts the transformation process on the inside of us. It is the repetition of making right decisions and living by the Word of God that produces permanent results. Discipline is comprised of small wins that lead to big successes. Winners understand that the little things matter. They understand that small adjustments over time, make a big difference and that greatness is comprised of a bunch of small moments handled well. When we consistently do things God's way, it builds and solidifies our godly blueprint and creates discipline. Once we develop discipline in one area of our life, it will eventually begin to spread into others.

In John chapter 14, verse 21 it says, *"Whoever has my commands and keeps them is the one who loves me. The one who loves me will be loved by my Father, and I too will love them and show myself to them."*

In this verse, God tells us that when we obey Him, we show Him that we love Him. When we obey His commandments, we show Him we want to experience the fullness of who He is.

The tricky thing about obedience is that God doesn't want us to obey Him out of obligation or fear. He wants us to obey Him out of love and trust.

Just like in a romantic relationship, you are first pursued and courted. After a couple of dates, if it's a good match, you start to develop feelings for the person. As you spend more time together, you learn about the individual's character and eventually begin to trust them. This trust develops into deep affection and sometimes, it turns to love. Trust cultivates love. Trust strengthens and nurtures love, so it can grow to new levels. Trust is the foundation for every loving relationship.

The same is true for our relationship with God. He pursued us from the very beginning. The Bible says in 1 John chapter 4, verse 19, *"We love Him because He loved us first."* God made the first move. And once we let Him in, it takes time for us to fall head-over-heels for Him, but everything begins with trust.

It is in the process of getting to know, trust and love Him, that we develop discipline and the genuine desire to obey.

Humility Is The Key

If trust is the flour, then humility is the yeast. Humility is the key ingredient that makes it all possible. Flour might be the recognizable substance of bread, but you can't bake it without yeast!

A humble mind and heart is the foundation to learning how to trust and obey God. A lack of humility will always distort your ability to hear His voice. A lack of humility will also affect the way you receive, process and understand His instructions.

Humility is the key to growing and maturing in Christ. Without it, we simply miss the mark. The opposite of humility is being prideful. And pride is a blessing blocker. It spiritually blinds us and prevents us from "seeing" what we need to see so that we can go where God wants us to go, and do what He has called us to do. Pride always insists on having its own way. It acts like a venom that kills trust in God and promotes trust in self.

This means that to be humble, we will have to set our personal agendas aside many times, trusting that God has our back. Trust and humility go hand-in-hand.

I once had a client that was struggling with following through on her work assignments and managing time. She left many projects uncompleted and made many commitments she did not keep. Her habits became a blessing blocker to her life and business. It was affecting her emotionally and financially.

As a result, she stopped believing in herself. She would even pass on amazing opportunities because she felt like she didn't have what it took. As part of her coaching, I gave her some homework. I asked her to write letters to the people she felt like had been affected the most by her behavior.

The main objective of this *homework* was for her to take responsibility for her actions and to clear her heart space with God, herself and others. It was time for her to move forward.

So, she found courage and wrote the letters by faith!

As she began to send out the letters, she noticed something very special. Her humility dismantled the guilt and shame she had been feeling for years about missing the mark. Once she opened her heart to people, apologized and admitted her shortcomings the weight on her shoulders left. She was now free to embrace who she was created to be.

And with every response she got from those letters, her heart would heal even more. Her humility gave people the opportunity to extend her grace. To honor that grace, she had to become more disciplined and work on keeping her commitments.

That is exactly how God works with us.

Do you trust Him enough to change and correct you? Will you humble yourself? Do you believe that His grace is sufficient?

When the answer to both of those questions is *yes* there are no limits to what you can accomplish!

Earlier in this chapter, we read Proverbs chapter 3, verse 12 which talked about God's correction coming out of His love for us as a father. But if we look at the verse before that, it says, *"My child, don't reject the Lord's discipline, and don't be upset when he corrects you."*

Proverbs chapter 12, verse 1 is another example of this but it goes even a little further. It shifts the focus from "do not reject" and takes it to "you must love it." The verse says, *"to learn, you must love discipline, it is stupid to hate correction."*

Humility is the key that unlocks all our trust issues with God, which allows us to a place where we can receive his discipline. If you believe and trust that God is good, you will obey Him from a place of faith and not fear. Once you understand this and decide to live by it, you will have access to new realms of opportunity. Humility is an essential characteristic of a true godly individual. Being humble means recognizing our total inability to accomplish anything apart from God.

Let's read more about God's perspective on discipline in Hebrews chapter 12 verses 4 through 11:

God Disciplines His Children
4 In your struggle against sin, you have not yet resisted to the point of shedding your blood. 5 And have you completely forgotten this word of encouragement that addresses you as a father addresses his son? It says,

"My son, do not make light of the Lord's discipline, and do not lose heart when he rebukes you, 6 because the Lord disciplines the one he loves, and he chastens everyone he accepts as his son."

7 Endure hardship as discipline; God is treating you as his children. For what children are not disciplined by their father? 8 If *you are not disciplined—and everyone undergoes discipline—then you are not legitimate, not true sons and daughters at all. 9 Moreover, we have all had human fathers who disciplined us and we respected them for it. How much more should we **submit** to the Father of spirits and live! 10 They disciplined us for a little while as they thought best; but God disciplines us for our good, in order that we may share in his holiness.*

Submission to God's authority is the pathway of personal humility. Nothing is more unpleasant than encountering someone who claims to be a follower of Jesus Christ, but they operate in spiritual pride. Nothing is more attractive to God than our humility.

God loves us first, then we learn to love Him and develop the discipline required to live our best lives according to His Word. It's our humility that promotes trust and it's our trust that provokes love. It is when we connect the dots to these three principles, that we encounter the true, living God and position ourselves for His purposes.

The Root

One time, I spoke to the young adults at my church. My message was called "The Triple Threat: Impact, Income and Influence." I did a live demonstration on stage and used the process of making coffee as an example to show how discipline is developed in our lives. Here are the steps I took the audience through:

1. We start off as plain and simple coffee beans, which are not necessarily that interesting.

2. Then we are smashed and go through a grinding process. This is the way we die to our personal motives and agenda. We die to our flesh and conform our lives

to the Word of God.

3. After that, we get packaged into a bag that contains and shapes us. This *"package"* is the place where, what we do and say fully aligns with the Word of God. This is the place where our integrity is formed and becomes solid.

4. Finally, we get put into the machine of life, a.k.a., the coffee maker, and hot water is poured through our now *solidified integrity.* The hot water representing the issues of life. As the water filters through our integrity, *"coffee is produced."* That coffee is *flavored* discipline.

Chances are, if you lack discipline, then your integrity will suffer from a deficit as well. These two go together. They are what I like to call "sister friends" to each other.

The Bible says in Lamentations Chapter 3, verse 40, *"Let us examine our ways and test them, and let us return to the Lord."* Therefore, if you need more discipline in your life, you should start by putting your integrity under the microscope of the Holy Spirit. Allow Him to search your heart and reveal to you, where how you live and what you say are out of alignment.

The more we bridge the gap between what we say and do, the harder it will be for the enemy to access our lives. This is because we are closing the gateway – the space through which he finds his entry. The devil is like a small, sneaky rodent that crawls through any opening it can find. He doesn't need a whole bunch of room to invade your life. He just needs a little *space.*

When your integrity is compromised, whether it is by lying to your spouse, deceiving a co-worker, missing deadlines, or repeatedly arriving late to your appointments, it creates a *space* through which the enemy can have access to your life.

The enemy comes to kill, steal and destroy (John 10:10). He prowls around like a roaring lion looking for someone to devour (1 Peter 5:8).

Embracing Grace for Humility And Discipline

Discipline, trust, humility, integrity. It can all sound a little bit overwhelming when you put them all together. But, the truth is, we don't have to do it all on our own. Thank God for grace!

We are works in progress. As you embark upon the journey of developing more discipline, take comfort in knowing that He who started a good work in you, is faithful to complete it.

If you commit to the process of transformation, God will completely transform you and every area of your life. There have been so many different times in my life that I have missed the mark and fell short of doing the very things that I am writing about, but the Bible tells us that we have all sinned and fallen short of the glory of God (Romans 3:23). His grace is sufficient for every shortcoming and every situation we have and will ever face. He is faithful. He will meet you where you are, and then carry you through to where He wants you to be. Be encouraged! He is creative, and He knows just how to get your attention.

He knows each one of us individually and intimately. He knows when and how we need to be helped. He understands our strengths and weaknesses. He has seen our backgrounds and our upbringings. He is familiar with our personalities and our potential. That is the beauty of God! So, every time He makes a move in our life or exposes an area that we need to develop in, we can rest assured that it is in our best interest.

Let's read Psalm chapter 139, verses 1 to 6:

1 O Lord, you have examined my heart
  and know everything about me.
2 You know when I sit down or stand up.
  You know my thoughts even when I'm far away.
3 You see me when I travel
  and when I rest at home.
  You know everything I do.
4 You know what I am going to say
  even before I say it, Lord.
5 You go before me and follow me.
  You place your hand of blessing on my head.
6 Such knowledge is too wonderful for me,
  too great for me to understand!

See! God knows you. In Him, nothing can be hidden. He knows exactly where He is taking you and He knows the level of discipline required to keep you there.

It's just like how cooking great food only comes from knowing your way around the kitchen. God is the Master Chef! He knows the who, what, when, where, why and how of deepening and developing your character. He knows how to combine the right ingredients to create the perfect recipe and produce the best taste.

God will never burn you! I know it may feel like He has forgotten you at times or that the temperatures of life are just too high, but He knows what He is doing.

Developing more discipline and growing up spiritually can be *tough* and it doesn't always feel good, but trust and believe that it's always for your good.

In Hebrews chapter 12, verse 11, the Bible says, *"No discipline is enjoyable while it is happening—it's painful! But afterward there will be a peaceful harvest of right living for those who are trained in this way."* And in Deuteronomy chapter 8, verse 5 says, *"Just as a parent disciplines a child, the Lord your God disciplines you for your own good."*

Discipline yields the harvest of an abundant life.

Don't Get Trapped!

Where there is no discipline, there can be no progress, and over the years of working with a variety of different clients, I have seen two mindsets that do significant damage in people's life and business. These mindsets are traps that keep people from being truly productive and reaching peak performance. They are the "Spirit of Entitlement" and "Spiritual Laziness". These are both spiritual conditions that result in living a life on the sidelines. They are traps that the enemy uses to keep people running around in circles, wondering why they haven't progressed much or witnessed the results they've set out to accomplish. Although, confronting these types of mindsets and behaviors can be uncomfortable and challenging, it is necessary, if we want to break free. If we choose to overlook such conditions, we will only remain stuck and stagnant. We must be careful not to get trapped in the revolving doors of the devil's tricks. It will only cause us to regress as followers of Christ and delay our destiny. We must break free!

When people lack discipline, a lot of the time it could be derived from carrying one of these two mindsets. If a person was spoiled growing up and they got everything they ever wanted, when they wanted it, and how they wanted it, often and unknowingly, they develop a *"Spirit of Entitlement."* This makes them subconsciously believe and behave with the expectation that people should always accommodate them and their needs. This is an unrealistic expectation. Then there is *"Spiritual Laziness"*. It sneaks up on people after a series of disappointments and they lose their will to win. They become overwhelmed about what it takes to fight back. Operating with either mindset will cause breakdowns in various areas of life. They will cause us to settle until we become self-spectators.

The language associated with someone operating with a "Spirit of Entitlement" is, *"I am entitled to this," "I deserve a promotion," "you own me this raise,"* and *"I owe it to myself."*

Entitlement embodies two attitudes. First, it embodies the idea *I am exempt from responsibility.* And second, it embodies the idea *I am owed special treatment.* In other words, I don't have to deal with my own issues and I should be treated better than others around me. You know, because I'm special.

People that live with this type of attitude feel that they deserve special treatment without taking on any responsibility. They often mismanage the grace card and abuse people's trust. The worst part is, they not only miss the mark many times, without owning their mistakes, but they also expect celebration for accomplishments that other people may perceive as normal day-to-day tasks. The root of entitlement is *selfishness.*

The essence of entitlement sends the message that *YOU* are the most important thing and topic in every moment. It creates a self-centered and self-focused person. It makes you believe that God owes you something and He doesn't. It shifts your life from being God-centered, to you being at the center of everything. It reduces God to someone that just helps you to get what you want and whatever you think you have a "right" to.

Someone struggling with "spiritual laziness" is an expert at making excuses. They usually have a reason for why things should be done tomorrow, why things are not finished, why things are too hard, too far, too complicated, too difficult...just too much! For a spiritually lazy person, an obstacle is something that provides them with an excuse to avoid any effort of any kind. For a diligent person, an obstacle is something that forces them to figure out another way of getting the job done. They see opportunity in opposition and overcome obstacles to achieve success.

Spiritual laziness will make you resist anything that requires effort and only make you want to participate in activities that are self-indulgent and distraction worthy. Ultimately, anything opposite of accomplishment, effort or service. This mindset will make you waste time, money, talent, and opportunities by under using them, improperly using them or not using them at all.

Consequences Of Spiritual Laziness

1. Spiritual Laziness leads to Poverty

Proverbs 10:4 - Lazy hands make for poverty, but diligent hands bring wealth.

Not just spiritual poverty but emotional and physical poverty as well.

2. Spiritual Laziness leads to Shame

Proverbs 10:5 - A wise youth harvests in the summer, but one who sleeps during harvest is a disgrace.

An unorganized life caused by Spiritual Laziness brings shame because when the "ball is dropped" and people become disappointment due to missed deadlines, commitments or whatever the case might be, over time it will begin to foster guilt.

3. **Spiritual Laziness leads to Depression**

Proverbs 13:4 - Lazy people want much but get little, but those who work hard will prosper.

Spiritual laziness is a thief. It robs a person of the many joys in life that others experience. Spiritually lazy people that don't acknowledge the truth grow envious of others and eventually become depressed about their own situation and condition.

4. **Spiritual Laziness leads to Debt**

Proverbs 12:24 - Work hard and become a leader; be lazy and become a slave.

Spiritually lazy people want things, but become indebted (slaves) to others for them. It takes little to no effort at all to create debt, but it takes energy, faith and a strategic effort to pay it off. Not all people in debt are spiritually lazy, but most spiritually lazy people end up being indebted financially, emotionally, and spiritually.

Proverbs chapter 18, verse 9 says, *"Whoever is lazy regarding his work is also a brother to the master of destruction."*

Spiritual laziness is like a deadly disease. It eats away at the fruit of your life, until it destroys it. Thank God there is a cure for it though! Believe it or not, it's not just the discipline of praying and reading your bible that's the cure, but that discipline comes from the cure, and that cure is our faithfulness. When we stand on the truth of God's word, lovingly serving him and others and making sure that he is the center of our everyday life. We are demonstrating our faithfulness. It's our steadfast adherence and our wholehearted devotion to Him and His word, that produces discipline.

If God leads you to confront your lack of discipline, whether it's because of a *spirit of entitlement* or *spiritual laziness*, don't get discouraged. Embrace it! God's grace will be sufficient, and He will carry you through. Simply, confess your faults, repent and keep it moving!

When God is cultivating your discipline, He will work in you and, simultaneously, move you forward in the plan He has for your life. God can do everything and be everywhere at once.

Isn't that amazing?

A couple of years ago, I did a lot of work in the arts and entertainment industry. I acted in commercials and hosted tv programs. As my career in the arts developed, many of my self-image insecurities were brought to the surface. I noticed there were several things that bothered me and made me feel self-conscious in front of the camera. I felt most insecure about my skin, hair, and my weight.

I had acne for most of my teenage years and it left me with a face full of dark spots and scars. My hair was super damaged from all the hairstyles and hair products I experimented with. And I gained weight from all that late-night pizza I devoured in college.

Because I felt so bad about the way I looked, I would make up excuses to give my agent for why I had to miss auditions.

One day, I got fed up with myself. I was tired of playing small and sabotaging my success. So, I sat down and wrote out a prayer to God. I cried out to Him and told Him how insecure I felt. I asked Him to help me lose weight, improve the condition of my skin and hair. I wanted help in all those areas.

I prayed to God and said:

Lord, I need your help. I am tired of living beneath my potential and giving up on myself. I am tired of being afraid. I know you want me to be healthy, but I don't know how to do it. I want to change my body and I want to develop better eating and exercising habits. I know you are calling me higher and if you help me in this area, I promise that I will start showing up and that I will never make up another excuse when you open doors for me.

I was certainly not expecting what happened next. But you know, God is funny like that.

The very next day I got a call from my agent. Her exact words were, *"Hi Ashley, how are you? I need to know if you are still plump."*

To which I replied, *"Plump?"*

She then said, *"Yes, plump! I asked because a fitness company wants to pay you to lose weight. They saw your picture and they want to use you for a print and media buy out."*

I woke up the next morning and went to the audition. There were eleven different casting directors and agents in the room with me, while auditioning for the part.

Can you imagine? Just the night before I had confessed to God my deepest feelings of insecurity and now I am standing in front of eleven strangers with a sports bra on and some spandex shorts! Talk about God having a sense of humor! Was this His way of helping me lose weight?

As I stood there, spandex on and belly out. They said, *"Ok Ashley, tell us a little about your eating habits?"*

I started talking and the more I shared, the more they would laugh. I guess my transparency was amusing. I never thought my eating habits and exercise stories were standup comedy material, but oh well! I shared my truth and they got some laughs out of it.

After the audition, guess what I did? I went and got some food. All that discomfort worked up my appetite.

And as I was sitting in the restaurant, eating up my meal, I got a call back from my agent. And she said, "Hi Ashley, I am so happy, they loved you, they thought you were so funny. They want you back!"

I went on a second audition and they gave me the part.

They paid me $10,000 to lose weight! I was given a personal trainer, a nutritionist, a free gym membership, and workout clothes. There were also a few other perks thrown in my contract as well.

Hallelujah, praise God!

He answered my prayer.

But regardless of the money and the personal trainer, this was still not going to be an easy task. I had never worked out before and I later found out that this was going to be a National Advertising Campaign. So, pictures of my *"plump"* body were going to be everywhere!

So, for 60 days, this was my drill. I had to get up, put on a swimsuit they picked out, take a front and profile picture with the camera they installed in my house. Then I had to take a train and two buses just to get to the gym. There, I would meet with my trainer and nutritionist. After, the workout while I was still hot and sweating with my hair looking a mess they would come to me with cameras pointing to my face asking, *"Hey Ashley, how was your workout?"*

I went from a size 12 to a size 6 in 60 days.

And this is how God first started teaching me about discipline! There has been such an amazing harvest produced from my original prayer. I not only lost the weight, but I learned to eat better and exercise regularly. During that process, I had to wake up, get ready, take the bus to meet my trainer, work out and work hard, then had to take the bus back, shower and change, and then get on with my day. On top of that, I was constantly listening to my trainer. I was told what to eat and when to eat. How much I had to exercise and stay focused on the goal. It was hard to give up my personal wants, but being forced to take the hard path is what gave me the enlightenment of being disciplined. This completely relates to how we grow spiritually and develop discipline in our walk with God, and I think we can all relate to that!

I, now, many years later, still go to the gym 4 to 5 times a week *without* the cameras. As a result, I have been able to help other women break free in this same area of their lives.

Glory to God!

It all started with an earnest prayer. Never discount the value of prayer and being vulnerable with God. He cares about every detail of your life. Even the *small* stuff!

Discipline is something we all need to develop to access the freedom that God has already provided for us. We need discipline to live a fruitful and fulfilled life. If you are struggling with being disciplined, fear not! You are completely able and equipped by God to overcome this struggle. The sins that come from a lack of discipline, are just some of the many sins that we all must deal with at one time or another. Some people are more prone to this type of sin just like some are more prone to anger or sexual sins.

God wants to help each one of us break free in the areas of our lives that are holding us back from being who He has called us to be. He wants us to be completely transformed into the image of Christ. No matter what you are struggling with, God will meet you where you are and help you move forward. *Remember, you are an overcomer!*

CHAPTER 8

HOW BAD DO YOU WANT IT?

Have you ever said this to someone, "I'm sorry, I promise I won't do that again," but you keep on doing it? I know I have. Maybe it was a promise that you made to your spouse, your children, your friend, or to yourself. Sometimes "it" happens again on accident or by genuine mistake. But, sometimes when it keeps on happening it can be because we have not taken the time to look within ourselves to discover the root of our behavior and or fully committed our full selves to the process of changing. We haven't turned on that switch in our heart that says I'm all in.

We've got one foot in the pool and the other one out. Now, how much swimming can get done like that? If you try to swim with one foot in the pool and the other one out, not only will you look like a crazy person, but you will probably also hurt yourself. If you are going to do some decent swimming, you must be all in. You won't get much accomplished if you've got one foot in your marriage and the other one out. You won't be very successful if you've got one foot in your business and the other one out. You have to be all in if you are going to become the best version of yourself and see all the wonderful plans and promises of God fulfilled in your life.

You might have said to yourself, "I'm ready to change my life!" But are you *really* all in?

Are you ready to apologize? Get up earlier? Make a budget? Pray More Often? Forgive?

Knowing that you need a change is simply not enough, you must be willing to take action. Your destiny is wrapped up in your decisions. Choose wisely.

My prayer for you, as you are reading this book, is that you will live with an all-in mentality. I pray that you won't live the watered-down version of your life and end up wondering what could have been. That you will have the courage to pursue purpose and the strength to persevere when life gets tough.

Do The Work

Whenever people refuse to change the behaviors that keep them stuck and stagnant, they will always find themselves repeating the same cycles. I have given several examples of these behavioral patterns and mindsets throughout this book. We all have the capacity to break free from the internal barriers that try to keep us from living our best lives! In order to do so, we must be willing to *do the work*. Don't be afraid of doing whatever it takes to break the cycle! We live in a right now society where everyone wants it quick, fast, and in a hurry. As a result, many people are settling for less than God's best and stopping short of the finish line. Meaning, they are only willing to put in enough work to get out of the pit, but not necessarily enough to live in the palace. They will do what it takes to pay off the bills but not enough to build wealth. I think you get where I am going with this. They are stuck in the in-between of life, afraid to take that next step, make that phone call or whatever it is. Success belongs to the ones who feel the fear, but *do the work* anyway! They are willing to do whatever it takes to get from where they are, to where they want to be. Are you?

Going from Rags To Riches Takes Work.

Having good ideas is easy, but executing them requires a different level of commitment and consistency. Building a computer takes skill. But turning that one computer into a company like Apple Inc., is a whole different story.

When you read or watch interviews about successful people, you will find they all have one thing in common when responding to questions about how they made it to the top. They usually say things like, "I got my first manuscript turned down 15 times before I finally got an editorial house to even notice me," "I was laid off from two different companies, before building the company you see here today," and "I was on the bench for years before I ever got a chance to play professionally."

The Key To Success Is Endurance. Successful People Don't Give Up!

Most people set goals for themselves, but end up showing that they are more committed to their past or their patterns than they are to their progress and potential. They are more committed to self-pity than to self-improvement. They want to excel in their purpose, but they don't want to partner with God to achieve the results.

Let's say I was committed to writing this book every night at 9 o'clock. But when the time comes, I get distracted, make myself a sandwich and start talking on the phone. That would communicate and prove that I was more committed to socializing that I was to obeying God and writing the book. If I had allowed myself to get distracted enough times, you would not even be reading this chapter.

To do the work, we also need to discover the real motivation behind our actions. When you know why you are doing something, it is easier to stay committed during the tough times.

So, maybe I haven't been able to sleep all the hours I would like to but I'm starting my own business and that requires an effort. Suddenly, the sacrifice of having fewer hours of sleep is worth the effort. Maybe I was not able to buy that cute dress I wanted because I was saving money to go on a trip. But simply thinking of that wonderful vacation ahead of me, made the dress so unnecessary. Keeping your goals in perspective, will always help you stay on track.

Many people can and have written books to help people transform their lives. God told me to write this one. I could have said "no" and God would still love me the same. But, I would have missed out on the blessings that came with stepping out on faith and writing it. And not just blessings for me but for whoever benefits from reading it.

When I started writing this book, I had a clear Why. God's job was to provide the How. I knew God led me to do it. And He promised that He would bring the readers deliverance and breakthrough. Keeping that in mind, I pressed forward toward the goal and trusted God for the results.

I had many opportunities to give up. I faced many challenges, especially when I was so close to finishing. Things would seem to take longer, and I would feel more distracted than when I began. Suddenly, I would look up, and before I knew it, a week had passed by before my eyes. I wouldn't even have gotten through a chapter! There were days I was discouraged and wanted to give up. I told you earlier in the book, that I didn't like writing very much, but it was me being able to keep God's love, and his promises to me at the center of my heart that kept me going, along with my "why" for writing it- you, the reader, my "why", and my ability to "see" the end. That is what allowed me to persevere.

Your why is the encouragement to your commitment. Do whatever it takes to remind yourself of why your goal is so important. Some people need to make note cards, others need to put reminders on their mirrors, figure out what works for you and do it.

Pray and involve God in every part of the process. You are not meant to do this on your own, God is there to help you. Find scriptures that support what you are working on. If you are working on improving the way you manage your finances, find some scriptures about money and being a good steward. If you are working on being secure, find some scriptures about your identity in Christ. I included a few below as examples.

Forgiving Yourself & Others
Matthew 6:14-15
Romans 12:16-18
Colossians 3:12-13
Ephesians 4:31

Health & Healing
Exodus 15:6
Isaiah 53:4-5
Jeremiah 30:17
2 Proverbs 4:20-22

Transforming Your Thinking
Romans 12:2
Philippians 4:8
Colossians 3:2-5
Ephesians 4:22-23

Watching What You Say
Ephesians 5:4,
2 Timothy 2:16
James 3:6
Colossians 4:6

Financial Stewardship
Luke 6:38
Deuteronomy 8:18
Psalm 115:14 -15
Matthew 6:24

Overcoming Fear & Insecurities
Psalm 56: 3-5
2 Timothy 1:7
Hebrews 2:15
Philippians 4:6-9

No matter what you are dealing with, you can always tap into the truth of God's Word, to get the proper perspective on any subject in your life. This is the best way to program your subconscious for success when life tries to move you in the opposite direction of your goals and God's purposes for your life.

If you need help or guidance in setting your goals with scripture being your foundation, please visit: http://breakfreebeunstoppable.com/unlockandunleash

Hebrews chapter 12, verses 1 and 2 say, *"Therefore, since we are surrounded by such a great cloud of witnesses, let us throw off everything that hinders and the sin that so easily entangles. And let us run with perseverance the race marked out for us, fixing our eyes on Jesus, the pioneer and perfecter of faith. For the joy set before him he endured the cross, scorning its shame, and sat down at the right hand of the throne of God."*

This is a race and when you focus on Jesus as the final destination of your faith, every effort along the way, becomes worth it. Suddenly being obedient, consistent, and denying yourself to follow God, stops being a burden.

Keeping your eyes on Jesus and The Cross reminds you that your spiritual journey is about eternal life, not about momentary comfort.

As you strive to accomplish your goals, keep your "Why" in front of you. Why are you committed to this goal and what will happen if this goal is never met? Weigh the consequences of not cutting it.

Some consequences are easier to deal with than others.

But what if the consequence had more eternal relevance?
What if you never talked to that one person about Jesus? What if you were meant to help them grow closer to God? Let's get one thing straight, God can certainly do it without you, but wouldn't you want to be a part of God's plans for you?

One Saturday night, a friend of mine was driving home. As she was driving, she prayed and asked God to work in certain areas of her life. As she was praying, she felt prompted to pray for the power to heal the sick. Suddenly, there was a massive car crash right in front of her. She heard a woman screaming for help. She had a choice. She could simply call an ambulance, or she could exercise her faith and get involved. She got out of the car and started praying for healing. She decided to do the work by choosing the second option. She positioned herself to be used by God and see His hand move in this situation.

I am happy to say that beyond all the negative doctor's reports, the people from that car accident were supernaturally healed! God could have healed them without my friend's efforts, but she would have missed out on the opportunity to see the miraculous power of God in action. This event led to strengthening not only her faith but the faith of those around her.

As children of God, when we commit to doing the work and staying consistent, it not only impacts our destiny but the lives of everyone we encounter along the way.

That's why we must be honest with ourselves about our level of commitment and consistency when it comes to accomplishing our goals and living out the plans of God. I have worked with many individuals that were frustrated because they were not seeing results in their life. And at some point, all of them had to come to a place where they came to the end of themselves and recognized that they needed to change.

It is easy to articulate what you want from God, but are you actually willing to do the work necessary to receive it. When I say do the work, I am talking about both the internal and external processes that position you to receive God's best.

For example, if you want to have a better relationship with one of your siblings, you must become intentional about loving them, forgiving them, spending time with them or whatever "it" is to see improvements. If you want to be a wealthy person, then you need to become more comfortable taking financial risks and develop more disciplined spending habits.

If you set a goal to quit smoking, you need to exercise self-control when deciding how you will maintain being smoke-free. If you desire to be married, your actions must demonstrate that you are more committed to purpose and personal development than you are to the attention of others or being promiscuous. Ouch! I know you didn't expect me to say that one, but it's true.

Doing the work is a process. You will not see results overnight. Just like if you stop eating donuts on Tuesday, you won't be a size 2 on Thursday. Be patient with yourself and take it one step at a time. Focus on your today and God will handle your tomorrow.

I don't know the specific areas of your character and life that God is calling you to improve but I encourage you to act immediately. Be honest with yourself, no matter how difficult, and make a quality decision to take steps toward reaching whatever that next level is for your life. God gave you the power, will, and strength to do this, so just know when things seem difficult, you are not alone in your battle.

God will always be by your side to teach, encourage, and guide you! But, it's up to you to *do the work*.

Partnership With God

When we live thinking that we need to exchange performance for love, we are wasting our time and energy! God is not interested in our phoniness or in hearing us pray out the list of our latest accomplishments. He wants you to be vulnerable and honest. Simply put, he wants all of you! Being in partnership with God starts by having a real, loving relationship with him. After all, aren't the best relationships the ones you can be real in, the ones where you can show up authentically.

It is all about our relationship with God, not about tradition and religious rules. It was my relationship with God that eventually led me to attending church, and to everything else that has ever mattered in my life.

Of course, like any other relationship in our lives, we will have days where we feel closer to God and days we feel some distance. Even though God is not a person, there are waves in our relationship with him. Some days your spirit catches fire and it blazes like a torch, and other days you can't even get a spark.

Any good relationship helps you grow, challenges you and stretches you, but in the end of it, it will always make you into the best version of yourself. And that will lead you to build better friendships, a better family, a better business, a better life.

So, put God first and engage in a real relationship with him! That is the only way you can position your heart to enter into a partnership with God, and allow his plans to become yours. The Bible says in Proverbs 16, verse 3 to "Commit your actions to the Lord, and your plans will succeed." If you do what it's in your hands, God will do what is out of your hands. God does his part if you do the work of laboring in the Word.

We are not going to grow spiritually by our own strength. God will help us lift the load. We just have to follow him in faith and do our part: Mark 4, verse 31 and 32 explains this very clearly; again, he said, "What shall we say the kingdom of God is like, or what parable shall we use to describe it? It is like a mustard seed, which is the smallest of all seeds on earth. Yet when planted, it grows and becomes the largest of all garden plants, with such big branches that the birds can perch in its shade."

The Word of God knows what to do once it gets planted inside of our hearts. We just need to continue planting seeds. God will bring the results, as we obey him and step out on faith. It is him alone who brings forth our transformation.

God is there to help us succeed, but first we need to start moving forward. Some people think that because we are in partnership with God that we can just chill out. This is not true! We do have something to contribute to the equation. Our hard work is the work of being in His presence, reading the Word, praying, seeking after Him or doing whatever it is that He's asking us to do. Not from a place of stress, but from a supernatural rest that allows for the favor of God in your life.

The Bible says the meek shall inherit the earth. The word "meek" means submitted but it also means coachable.

As you enter into partnership with God you gain access to His promises. You have access to His peace, joy, love, and purpose. You also have access to a new life, a new heart, but that comes in with transformation and processes you will need to endure to receive God's best for you.

Just because you are in partnership with somebody, it doesn't mean you don't do any work. In the business world, when you come into partnership with someone, there are roles that each of you would have to play and the more that gets defined the better you can show up to the partnership. As we walk with God, we will better understand the roles we each play.

We should be thankful that through the Word of God, the role in our relationship with Him is already defined. And the best part is that you never have to worry about Him falling short, failing or abandoning you. He really is the perfect partner!

In a natural business relationship, the more you and your partner trust each other, the more you can advance together. If your partner worries about you spending the money or being irresponsible about your assignments, the business won't grow to its full potential. When you enter a trusting relationship with God, you get access to advance the Kingdom with Him.

"Whoever can be trusted with very little can also be trusted with much, and whoever is dishonest with very little will also be dishonest with much. (Luke 16:10)

God wants you to be a good steward of the things He puts in your hands. If you want to keep a good partnership with Him, you must do your part in keeping up your end. Just like you want trust in a relationship you must have trust with God. And God must be able to trust you. Besides, He is everywhere, God is not a partner you can cheat.

In this partnership though, there is someone leading and someone following. There is a big stakeholder. He always has the final vote. Can you figure out which one you are, and which one is God?

All In

If you discover that you are not "all in" with God or any other area of your life where you desire to see better results, you need to step out on faith and make the adjustments. God will meet you where you are and His grace will be sufficient enough for you to overcome.

I don't want you to deceive yourself by thinking that the promises of God are going to fall out of the sky. You must play your role and play it well in the process of heaven coming to Earth in all areas of your life. You must decide in your heart to be "all in" and then decide to "do the work."

The other day, I worked out with my personal trainer. I told him that I was concerned because although I could see my body shaping, my arms and legs toning up, my stomach did not seem to be improving. I could still see the muffin top I desperately wanted to disappear. He told me the same thing that he always tells me, "Ashley, fall in love with the process." In other words, just keep showing up and your stomach will go down if you continue to do the work.

Clearly, he sees clients all the time and can recognize if a body is on track or not. He knows if someone is working out in a way that will produce results or if they are working out with a minimum level of effort. He knows it's not about perfection, it's about progress. He understands that my ability to consistently show up and do the work will eventually yield a breakthrough. And the same is true for you in every area of your life!

Consistency = Breakthrough

If you are not consistent and you only do what you're supposed to do some of the time, you really can't get a quality result. Every time you get off track, it delays your arrival to your destiny. And if you continue down that path long enough, you will lose your progress altogether and find yourself right back where you started.

God made us self-programmable. Most of our behaviors are being dictated from our subconscious mind. If you don't reprogram your subconscious to align with the goals you desire to accomplish, you will not be able to achieve or maintain them. You must transform your thinking! Shout out to chapter 5!

You can have good intentions to do whatever you want in life. You can desire to grow spiritually, change your body, or start an organization, but if you don't do the work necessary in partnership with God, your intentions will not be enough to get you there.

Let's say you really want to grow closer to God. So, you go out and buy a devotional. You purchase a pack of highlighters and a nice new journal to write all your favorite verses and notes in. Then, you set an alarm on your phone and put your Bible right on top of the nightstand. Setting yourself up perfectly to spend some quality time with God in the morning. Although, you might have done an excellent job preparing yourself to spend time with Him, your new supplies and set alarm do not necessarily guarantee that you will get up and do it. Sometimes we put all our energy on the external components of change and neglect the internal process. Truth is, God prospers us from the inside out. So, if you can get your "inside" together, your "outside" will follow.

On our journey of life, there will always be a series of steps or actions that we need to take to see the promises of God fulfilled. I am sure you have heard this before, "You are not waiting on God, God is waiting on you." That's what being "all in" and "doing the work" is about. It's about you doing your part of the process. It's about showing up consistently. It's about giving God all you've got and actively living the truth long enough to see the results.

Climb Out Your Comfort Zone

Your comfort zone is a cage that starves your passion and suffocates your potential.

Your comfort zone provides an illusion of safety, when it's the complete opposite. Your comfort zone is the most dangerous enemy and the biggest threat to your destiny. It allows you to repeat the same routines and patterns repeatedly until you self-destruct or settle for less that God's best.

Your comfort zone arrests your spiritual and emotional development. It enables you to play small and then allows you to reward yourself for it. This creates a false reality because in your mind, you think you are moving forward, but you are really stuck in the same spot. It's like running a marathon versus running on a treadmill. You are moving your legs in both scenarios, but only one of them will take you to a finish line.

It is not uncommon to see Christians living like everyone else in the world: comfortable, passive, used to doing their same old routine day in and day out. But we were meant to move, to grow, and to transform, not only ourselves but the world around us. Trust and believe that there is nothing comfortable about being a Christian. I mean, what was comfortable about Jesus being crucified? Or about Peter walking on water? What about Jonah being in the belly of a fish or about Daniel being in a lion's den? Can you find any comfort in David killing Goliath or Noah building an arch? Let's think about Gideon leading an army or Mary giving birth as a virgin? Let's face it, there was nothing comfortable about any of those situations!

There is no comfort for our flesh when it comes to living boldly for Christ. It requires us to completely climb out of our comfort zone.

Living inside your comfort zone is the opposite of living in faith and for Christ. Unfortunately, many people live and die without ever leaving their comfort zone. I decree and declare, in the name of Jesus, that this will not be you!

As you are practicing the concepts in this book to become the best version of yourself, you will be confronted by your comfort zone. That pattern, person, place or thing in your life that tries to keep you stuck and makes you settle for playing small and living beneath your full potential.

Your comfort zone is the pattern, person, place, or thing that you bump into when you're trying to break through to the next level of life. And although the enemy will use his tricks and tactics to try and defeat you, your worst enemy many times can be yourself.

Only you know what that comfort zone is. It could be a relationship, occupation, bad habit, defeated mindset, or some other familiar set of circumstances. Whatever pops in your mind as you read this, probably is it. That thing you don't want to let go of or that thing you are afraid to do.

But if you really want to climb out of your comfort zone, you will need to be honest with yourself. That is the only way you will be able to tackle it straight on and with your full strength.

The truth is, whether we recognize it or not, we all have a comfort zone to tackle. For me, I had always been afraid of public speaking. Even though I was very talkative growing up! At one point my grandfather told me, "there is one thing you should never be afraid of doing Ashley. And that is talking." I guess that was his way of being funny!

Still, I would always feel self-conscious when speaking in front of larger groups. When I was a kid, I would avoid asking questions in class and internally begged not to be called on to read out loud. I was and have always been much more comfortable with small groups and one on one conversations.

Then, one night, right in the middle of my lovely and "comfortable" walk with Christ, I was called to speak to the young adults at my church. I had a decision to make, I could say, "no," and shrink back or I could step up to the plate and face my fear. I am happy to say through God's grace I could face my fear and I have been public speaking ever since. But In that moment, I was forced to climb out of my comfort zone.

This doesn't mean I am thrilled about public speaking now or that I don't freak out behind the scenes every time I am asked to step in front of an audience. But I now know that I can trust God to bring me through. I know that He won't set me up for failure. The same is true for you.

We must remind ourselves that He loves us and that if He leads us to walk on water or asks us to do something we don't feel qualified to do, it is because He sees something in us that we don't. Therefore, we can step out in faith, knowing that He will guide the way and provide everything we need in the process. You can do all things through Christ who strengthens you (Philippians 4:13).

But maybe, just like many others, you still can't quite well recognize your comfort zone. You might need to train yourself on how to spot it. Learning how to recognize it is step one. So, let's see some examples together. As you read this, search deep within yourself and ask the Holy Spirit to reveal to you your comfort zone.

It could be keeping the same job for years and years without growing professionally. Or staying in a "kind of good" relationship, out of fear of being alone or not meeting anyone new. It could be keeping your ideas to yourself, because of fear. Your comfort zone can also show up in behavioral patterns like being late, missing deadlines, eating the wrong foods, all because changing requires an effort you are unwilling to make. It can be dating people that are not good for you just because you got used to it and you know that to aim higher you need to put in some work on your part. It could even reflect on you hanging out only with people that act and think like you, so you never feel challenged.

Don't just climb out. Conquer your comfort zone. To do so, I have compiled a list of tips that will help you in the process:

Tips to Help You Conquer Your Comfort Zone:

1- Do what you are afraid of doing.
2- Find an accountability partner.
3- Switch up your daily routine in some way.
4- Pray and ask God to deliver you from your fears.
5- Join a group or participate in activities that challenge you.
6- Write a mission statement that reminds you of your "why."
7- Adjust your self-talk to match what the Word of God says.
8- Break your goal down into small steps.
9- Picture the worst-case scenario and put your fear in perspective.
10- Give yourself an ultimatum.

Be encouraged and know that God is with you. Put on your hiking gear and get to climbing!

Stick And Stay & Let It Pay

Never underestimate the power of consistency. When you operate with a steadfast adherence to the same principles, you will eventually witness a breakthrough. This doesn't always mean things will always go your way or that you will get the results you expected. But, if God is at the center of your life, you will get the results that perfectly match the destiny He has for you.

When you find a pattern, you want to change or a behavior you want to improve, keeping consistent in the process is crucial.

When I think about the word consistency, it always reminds me of something my grandfather used to say, "stick and stay and let it pay." One time, while we were sitting down and chatting, he was talking to me about the ins and outs of finances, investments and the stock market. He explained that as a person invests, they will see their portfolio fluctuate. Sometimes they will see their accounts multiplying and then other days they may see them drop drastically.

Then he added that regardless of all of that, when you see the accounts drop, you shouldn't freak out and withdraw all your investments out of fear. But that you should just ride the wave and be patient.

When you are certain that you chose a good stock to invest in then you should, "stick and stay and let it pay." And as you do the accounts will eventually balance out and you will reap a harvest.

I remember hearing him say this and thinking about how it applies to so many other situations. If we are consistent in our efforts in reaching our dreams and goals, it will pay off.

Allow your relationship with Christ to reap the rewards of your commitment. Although you will not always see the progress right away, God is always at work!

That is what living by faith looks like, with the advantage that we are already winners in Christ (Romans 8:31-39). But, to be able to live out of that victory, we need to trust God, endure the process and stay committed to Him and what He is telling us to do no matter what.

If Jesus is your focus and He continues to be the one that guides you and strengthens you, no goal is too big for you to accomplish.

Many people leave relationships too soon. They give up on the gym too soon. They quit their jobs too soon. Simply because they get discouraged in the process.

If you get into marriage thinking that if it gets too hard, you can always get a divorce, you will soon find a reason to break the marriage. But if you enter into it with a true and unconditional commitment in your heart, you will be better prepared to persevere during the trials and tribulations.

One of the times that required me to "stick and stay" in my life was the process of writing this book. I had to be consistent from cover to cover. I started this journey in the summer of August 2011. Back then it was me and my laptop sitting in the park next to my grandparent's house in Door County, Wisconsin. I was so full of excitement and joy. I had recently learned so much about God and I wanted to share what I discovered. I could also feel God pushing me to write. So, I gathered up some courage and began the process.

In the back of my mind though, I was not sure what would come of it. I couldn't even think about specific subjects to write about. I had titles, notes and a bunch of information. But the information was disjointed. Then, a writer friend of mine offered to help me. She was also a client of mine so she was familiar with my teachings. I told her I would happily accept her help, because to be honest, I had absolutely no idea what I was doing!

First, she interviewed me to pull more of the content out of me. She did so because at the beginning, I was much more comfortable speaking the content than I was writing it. But, still there was something missing. Although she had good intentions, I could discern that her heart was not fully committed and that she needed to focus on other projects in that season of her life. And although she was the right person to help me start, I knew she was not the right person to help me finish this journey.

So, we parted ways professionally and I struggled with the book on my own for a while. Eventually, I was ready for the next step. Editing my book. So, I registered for an online platform to search for an editor. After receiving a lot of applications, no one seem to fit. So, I decided to leave the job post open for one more day.

Then, at the last minute, one more applicant reached out to me. As soon as we corresponded, I knew she was a match for the project. She was a Christian woman from Costa Rica that served in the women's ministry at her church. I could tell from our correspondence, that English was not her first language, but we had a connection in the spirit and I knew it was God. I don't know exactly how to explain it with words, but I knew she was the person that I was supposed to hire. So, I did! We have been working together ever since.

So, I started the process of editing and writing the book again. She had a lot of experience with writing and she could pinpoint the areas of the chapters that needed more development and she pushed me to become a better writer. It was frustrating because I didn't really like writing in the first place and now here was this lady telling me that she wanted me to write more! Without her help, each chapter in this book would have only been two pages. I am known to be a direct communicator, so you would have read a title and then a straightforward paragraph on how to tackle that topic.

We went through a creative process for several months, of writing, editing, and adding stories. I was ready to announce to the world that my book was finally finished. When suddenly, God told me to reset!

Reset? I was like, "What? Reset? What does that mean God?"

He said, "Ashley, I need you to spiritually reset and consecrate yourself to me, and then, start over."

I immediately thought, "God you must be crazy, it is finished! The book is finished!!!"

And yes, the number of exclamation points is my way of communicating the level of frustration and disappointment I felt at that moment.

But I obeyed God and set my emotions aside. I started over. This is the book you are reading as a result.

In the beginning, I didn't understand why God had asked me to "reset." But looking back, I now understand that I had grown into a new level of spiritual maturity and He wanted me to share those stories and insights with you in this book. I had experienced a new level of healing in my heart, that opened me up to sharing stories that I was uncomfortable sharing in the past.

So, who knew that my process of writing this book would take 6 years? I sure didn't.

As you can tell from my experience, the process was a little hectic. I went through so many stages and challenges. But I learned within my process that consistency is about perseverance and progress, not about perfection.

And that is how God sees you and your break free journey. He just wants you to trust Him and keep going. Keep writing, keep believing, keep praying, keep seeking, keep growing. He wants you to take possession of your process. He wants you to become whole, all that He has called you to be. There are times when all of us tend to procrastinate, but thankfully, we have God to push us to the end of that finish line.

So, wherever God is leading you to invest your talent, time, or treasure, stick and stay and let it pay!

Celebrate Your Wins

People that know me closely and have seen me go through extremely challenging situations in life, have often asked how am I able to stay focused and "in action" when I feel discouraged or under pressure. The answer I often give is that I slow down and rehearse my victories in Christ. I remember and replay the times God has delivered me repeatedly to build my faith for the win. That is what gives me the strength to keep going.

In the process of practicing commitment and consistency it's important to celebrate your wins. Remember those moments when you recognize your growth and you finally break free from whatever has been holding you back will give you energy, strength, and hope for the journey.

Whether your breakthroughs are big or small, acknowledging them always allows you to see your progress within the process. There is nothing more frustrating or damaging than beating yourself up when you're undergoing change. You must learn to become your biggest fan.

Think about it. If one of your closest friends was going through a difficult time as they were trying to change. How would you treat them? Would you be the friend that constantly reminds them of their mistakes or the friend that motivates and inspires them to keep moving forward. Hopefully you would be friend number two. Learn to be that type of friend to yourself. Learn to celebrate yourself as a loving and supporting friend.

The reason why I keep using the word learn, is because this is something I believe many of us struggle with and need to learn how to do. Being kind to ourselves is crucial to our spiritual and emotional health. Especially during times of discomfort and seasons of growing pains.

In my life, I have had to work on this a lot. I tend to be hard on myself. A lot of it comes from my personality type and my natural desire to succeed. But some of it comes from how I was raised.

My mom always pushed me to be the best version of myself. She raised me with tough love. Looking back, I am extremely grateful for her ability to pull out my full potential and as result I now have the capacity to do this for myself. Although this quality in my character is a blessing that opens doors, enables me to serve with excellence and achieve optimal results, if mismanaged it can trip me up, discourage me and drive me into depression. Seeking perfection can lead us to a place of being spiritually paralyzed and defeated. Practicing consistency and not perfection leads us to results.

I have learned to overcome this issue by celebrating my milestones and asking for support.

I am results driven, and I tend to go from one accomplishment to another without ever stopping to savor them. Fortunately, God has blessed me with amazing friends who know that this is one of my weaknesses and they encourage me to celebrate every breakthrough, both big and small.

So, celebrate the five pounds you lost, before reaching your weight loss goal. Celebrate your interview, on your way to receiving a new job. Celebrate your first client, before your business has fully developed. Celebrate your wins and keep moving forward!

There is a reason why God asked His people in the Old Testament to build altars to commemorate the victories He had given them.

In 1 Samuel 17:37, David is presented with a very big challenge. Killing Goliath! And this is what he said: The Lord who rescued me from the paw of the lion and the paw of the bear will rescue me from the hand of this Philistine.

Remembering the battles God won for us ignites hope in our hearts to face new challenges. It gives us strength to keep moving forward, all the while knowing that He will remain faithful.

CHAPTER 9

OBEY AWAY

There have been multiple times in my life where I was going through a lot of challenges, mainly in relationships. Although some of the situations I faced had to do with what was going on with some of the people around me, I also knew God wanted to do a work in my heart. He kept showing me, "me" and the areas of my character that needed to develop.

God was taking me to another level and it required a deeper level of consecration and intimacy in my relationship with Him. I could no longer entertain certain connections and conversations because they were a hindrance to my spiritual growth. I needed to separate myself to really seek God.

This was painful and problematic because I really loved the people that God was asking me to walk away from. I had invested a lot of myself into these relationships and I didn't want to let them go. Maybe you can relate?

Nevertheless, I knew that for me to mature spiritually, I needed to obey his guidance. I didn't know exactly how to separate myself from these individuals because we had a lot of the same mutual friends. I was unsure of how to detach myself from them. So, I prayed and asked God to help me. This time, He responded to me by speaking through my spiritual mother, Pastor Barbara. Remember? I told you about her in chapter one. God guided me through another one of her catchy phrases.

I explained to her how God was telling me to move away from certain people and relationships. I shared my fears and frustrations about trusting God and the process. I was afraid of being misunderstood and judged. I was also afraid of being alone.

She asked me, "Well, what did God tell you to do exactly, Ashley?"

I explained that God was leading me to separate from certain individuals to seek Him in a deeper way, so I could enter the next dimension of my life.

I remember her looking at me, chuckling a little bit, and then finally saying, "Well then, obey away!"

From that moment on, the phrase stuck with me. It has now become the mantra for every major move I've had to make whenever God challenges me to let go of something, so that I can move forward.

Looking back, as painful as it was, I now understand why I needed to obey away from those relationships and individuals. I had to be willing to let go of my past to embrace my future.

Nature illustrates this concept for us perfectly. When the seasons change, trees go through a full transformation process.

In the spring, flowers and the leaves of a tree blossom with strength and bright colors. Then summer comes, and the sun shines bright, and you get to see a fuller expression of their beauty. After that, the cool crisp air of autumn falls, and the leaves begin to change colors and texture. Eventually, the wind comes and blows them off the branches. The once fully-blossomed trees are now baring for a while. The cold of winter arrives and everything from the prior seasons dies.

Then, a few months later, the cycle starts all over again. As we walk with God, this same process is reflected in our lives.

The trees would never produce new leaves and flowers, if the old ones didn't fall off. That is the circle of life. You can never get the new, hanging on to the old. The Bible says in Matthew chapter 9, verse 17, "Neither do people pour new wine into old wineskins. If they do, the skins will burst; the wine will run out and the wineskins will be ruined. No, they pour new wine into new wineskins, and both are preserved."

In Biblical times, the wine was not kept in glass bottles like we do today. Instead, it was poured into goat-skins sewn around the edges to form watertight bags. The new wine would begin to expand as it fermented, which would stretch the skin holding it. Once the wine aged properly, the expansion would stop. But if new wine was poured in, the process of expansion would begin again. Ultimately, causing the already stretched skins to burst.

Jesus knows what He wants to pour into us and He is not going to deposit anything new into the old. When we have thought patterns, habits, relationships or anything else that no longer serves His purposes for our life, He will ask us to obey away from them. He can't give us the new thing if we refuse to give up the old.

The problem is, we have the tendency to feed relationships and situations that no longer serve us and God's purposes for our life, simply because it feels familiar and comfortable. But remember, whatever you feed will eventually grow. And if you want to live your best life, you can't spend time watering seeds that God didn't plant. No matter how beautiful they may seem to be as they grow, if it is not God's will for your life, they will only produce a counterfeit harvest.

In Matthew chapter 13, verses 24 to 30, the Bible talks about the connection between wheat and weeds. It describes how they resemble each other as they grow side by side. And although they look very similar as they both blossom, weeds don't bear fruit. In fact, before you can even harvest the grains from the wheat, the weeds must be uprooted. The same is true for our lives. We must be willing to let go of the things that no longer serve us and God's purposes for our life if we want to harvest His best.

When we don't obey away, we end up wasting our time, talent and treasure on situations that are irrelevant to our future. We must be careful not to resuscitate and give life to the very things that God is trying to kill. Obeying away takes courage! It requires us to starve situations and relationships that God was never in or no longer endorses.

The practice of obeying away will look different for every person. It can look like you are staying away from friends that only knew you "back then" or not calling your ex because you know you will be tempted to have sex. It might look like not getting out of bed to have a second piece of cake. We are all different and God deals with each one of us in a personal way. He knows us intimately and understands deeply which parts of our lives need to be adjusted for us to become the best version of ourselves.

The Bible says in Isaiah chapter 1, verse 19, "if you are willing and obedient you will eat the good of the land." When Jesus saved us, He took away the weight of our sin. As a result, we have been set free and delivered from having to be "perfect" and doing everything "right". We have been made righteous because Christ is righteous. And our uprightness and virtue has more to do with who God is then how we are acting or behaving. His love for us is the foundation of his sacrifice. When we have a revelation of that, it allows us to understand how deeply we are loved and it makes it easier for us to obey him.

He said in John chapter 14, verse 21, "those who love me will keep my commandments and I will manifest myself to them." We can't say we love God if our actions prove otherwise. People sometimes wonder why they don't see the full manifestation of God's promises in their life, but they never stop to wonder if their obedience plays any role in it.

In my experiences as a coach, I get a lot of questions like, "why am I not married yet?" "Where is the new job I have been praying for?" "Why haven't I been promoted?" "Why hasn't God blessed me with more money?"

The more I work with my clients in these areas of their life and business, the more I notice the common denominators to these types of frustrations. Usually, after digging deep we discover they are operating with a blind spot. And a lot of times our blind spot is our lack of obedience.

It's like when you're driving on the expressway and your visibility of the car in the lane next to you is compromised. Although you still have 90% of the vision around you, missing that one spot can be risky. One bad move, or lack of proper estimation, could cost your life.

That is why it's so important for us to constantly take time to check in with the Holy Spirit and to allow Him to search our hearts and see if there is anything He wants us to obey away from.

You can't expect God to heal your heart if you're unwilling to break-off the relationship that hurt you. You can't expect God to restore your relationship with your mother, if you refuse to stop disrespecting her with your words.

Learning to obey away takes practice. Some days you will feel like you've mastered it and other days you will feel like you've failed miserably. It's all a part of the process. Keep in mind that we are all works in progress, so when you miss the mark, don't get discouraged. God's mercies are new every morning and He will give you the strength you need every step of the way.

Security Checkpoint

Every time you get close to breaking through to a new level in your life, you will experience what I like to call a security checkpoint. It is like the process in the airport prior to boarding a plane.

Before you can board the plane, you must pass the point of inspection. The place where they make you take off everything you are carrying, your baggage, your shoes, and anything that could potentially set off the security scanner.

There's a lot of taking off, before taking off. And during that process, there will be things that God will allow you to keep, like divine relationships. There will be things like un-forgiveness, old thinking and behavioral patterns that need to go in the garbage can. But there are some things that are so damaging, if you don't get rid of them, you can't go to the next level.

The purpose of the inspection is to make sure you are not carrying anything that could be potentially hazardous or cause danger to you or anyone around you as you head to your destination. They want to make sure you're safe to travel.

Every time you're going through the security checkpoint, there's a lot of commotion, and it is usually very uncomfortable. Let's face it, we don't like to take off our shoes and throw away our water or expensive lotion. The process is very uncomfortable for several reasons. One, because it's very detailed and it requires patience. You are not the only person in line and everyone is moving at a different pace. Two, they're making you surrender all your personal items, like your wallet, your purse, your watch and your phone. Not only that, but they're investigating each one of them. They are searching for things that can only be detected with specific equipment, technology and trained eyes.

Now, not only do your things go through the scanner, but then you go through one, too. And no one can go through that process with you. You go through it alone and without any of your stuff.

The security checkpoint is the same way God deals with us. He only lets us get so far before we are sent through an inspection. It's that place where He requires us to completely leave our emotional baggage, our past and our old ways of thinking. He asks us to lay down anything that could potentially damage or sabotage the plan He has for our lives.

He makes us give Him the things that we value the most to see how attached we are to them and if we are willing to trust Him. He searches the deepest parts of our hearts for motives. He separates us from the crowd and meticulously looks to see if we fully represent who He had in mind when He originally created us. Then, when He finally recognizes Himself in us, He allows us to pass the point of inspection and then moves us into our promise land.

I've been to the airport many times and there is one thing that usually makes the security checkpoint process run smoothly - obedience. When we follow the instructions given and willingly participate in the procedure, we can get through it faster. As we do this, it not only benefits us individually but it also positively impacts those around us. Obedience grants you access to your destiny. Our willingness to follow instructions will always determine whether we get delayed or if we are propelled.

Jesus obeyed to the point of death. That is how deep His obedience ran. You can't pray past obedience or fast-pass obedience. You can't meditate your way out of obedience or serve enough hours in church to override being obedient. If you are going to fulfill your God given purpose and receive everything that God has for you, then you must be willing to obey.

The Bible says in Deuteronomy chapter 28, verses 1 to 2, "if you fully obey the Lord your God and carefully follow all His commands I give you today, the Lord your God will set you high above all the nations on earth." Obedience guarantees your success. It doesn't mean that everything will go your way or look perfect in the process, but it is a promise. Obey God, take off your shoes, and pass your security checkpoint. Trust God and enjoy the flight to your next destination.

Submission Not Slavery

It's a privilege to obey God. Think about it. He has an amazing plan and purpose for our lives and provides everything we need to get there in the process. His love and power come with more insights, plans, resources and promises than we could ever fully understand. We all have the choice to participate in those plans or not. God has given us free will and therefore we are not obligated to obey Him or to participate in any of His plans.

However, we should want to. So, if this is the case and God has already provided us with all these amazing things, then why are some believers thriving while others are simply surviving?

I'm sure you have your own thoughts about that question. I have a few myself. I believe that many people who are living beneath their God given potential are doing so because they refuse to humble themselves consistently and obey God. They are too consumed with their own thoughts and feelings, everything they do is driven by one of two statements, "It's all about me" or "I know best." Their lack of submission is the root of their suffering.

Often, we think that obeying God is going to feel like a punishment, and that is why we don't submit. But God is not a drill sergeant. He is not walking around wearing army fatigues, blowing a whistle in our ears screaming, "give me 50 pushups!"

God is a loving father and He draws us. The devil tries to drive us. Do you know the difference? When God draws you, it feels like clues you are following to find hidden treasure. When you are being driven it feels like someone is dragging you by your ear or your collar around the room. God's love should draw you into submission. Unlike the opposite where you feel like you are being forced into it. We are not slaves for God. That was never the idea. We are His sons and daughters and He is madly in love with us. He sacrificed His only son, Jesus, so that we could have a relationship with Him. Not so that He could boss us around and tell us what to do.

When you are in a relationship with someone and you love them, it's your desire to please them. Our obedience pleases God and we should want to please him. It communicates not only that we love and trust Him, but also that we can be trusted. It is hard to love and trust someone you don't know. Many times, our perspective of obedience can be distorted because we don't truly know God. Our image of His character is dysfunctional because we put Him in the same category as people. The same people that have failed, hurt, or disappointed us. We see God through our foggy glasses of fear, pain, shame, guilt and rejection. Therefore, it makes us not want to obey him. We don't believe in our hearts that He is really for us. And as a result, we can resist submitting to Him and delay or neglect altogether, following His instructions. When you know that God loves you wholeheartedly, and you know that He is on your side, submission is no longer a chore, but a privilege.

It is important that you challenge your perspective of God, and make sure that you are seeing Him clearly. Because how you perceive God has everything to do with what you will be able to receive from Him and who He will be in your life. For example, you can't be healed if you don't perceive Him as a healer. You can't live in abundance and overflow if you don't know Him as a provider. You'll never feel secure or safe if you don't see Him as a protector. And you will always be stuck and stagnant, operating in fear if you don't recognize Him as the author and finisher of your faith! Having the correct perception of God is what releases His power.

And our obedience to God will always be dependent upon us having the right perspective.

Counterfeit obedience is when we create our own opportunities, do things our way — and then say it was God.

When we refuse to obey God, we sin and keep on sinning. When we refuse God, we refuse to submit and acknowledge our sins, hurts, anger, and agendas. We refuse to repent and grow from them. And over time that hardens our hearts and leads us away from God.

Many times, this unwillingness to submit comes from the fear and insecurities that arise when we think we are "missing" something or we have "unmet expectations." In both cases, if not properly redefined and checked, these thoughts can lead us down a path of destruction through disobedience. When we see ourselves as "inferior" or "without" or in "lack" it opens the door for us to be deceived and led astray. It creates space for the enemy to enter in and steal from our lives.

On the other hand, when we obey away and develop the maturity to deny ourselves to follow the Will of God, we grow into the best version of ourselves. We break through to new levels, where we let go of our pride and the ways of the world. As a result, our faith stands firm!

In James chapter 4, verses 6 to 8, the Bible tells us this:

"God opposes the proud but shows favor to the humble. Submit yourselves, then, to God. Resist the devil, and he will flee from you. Come near to God and he will come near to you."

So, when we are prideful, it blocks us from God's best. It impairs our vision, as I mentioned previously, so that we can't see what God has in store for us. Humility is the gateway to real submission and obedience.

God requires us to humble ourselves and surrender to Him in all areas of our lives, not just in some. We must submit our thoughts, emotions, body, relationships, finances, and work, to God. When we do this, we secure our victory.

The amazing thing about the process of yielding and submitting to God, is that resisting temptation becomes less of a struggle as we do it. Many times, people try to resist the devil without first submitting to God. It doesn't work that way!

It is like trying to eat dinner at a restaurant before you even order. Or trying to take a shower without turning on the water. Submission and resisting are two sides of the same coin, you can't have one without the other. Your success as a believer will always be determined by your level of submission and your ability to resist temptation.

It is important keep to in mind that God wants us to obey away, out of love, not fear or obligation. It's like doing the dishes in your house when you were growing up. Our parents didn't want us to do them with a poor attitude or just because they asked us to. They wanted us to help around the house as a way of showing love and gratitude.

Similarly, our obedience should be rooted in our love for God and our ability to trust Him. The level at which we know Him will always be reflected through our willingness to submit.

It's like when you were little, and your mom said, "don't touch the stove."

Even if you didn't realize how hot the stove was, you had a choice to make. You could choose to trust your mother or find out how hot the stove really was by touching it and potentially getting burned in the process.

When we don't trust the judgement of another person, it is hard to trust their advice or instructions. The same is true in our relationship with God. We won't trust Him if we don't think He has our best interests at heart.

When we trust and love God, we can show it by being willing to surrender our will to Him. This communicates to the Lord that His Word carries weight in our lives and that we're unwilling to just do our own thing. Trusting and loving God is about more than just words; it's about the decisions we make daily and the motives behind them.

Jesus obeyed his Father to the point of death for the sake of the world, and we are called to obey God as a response to the love we received on the cross.

The beautiful thing about this is, after we start to live with obedience at the center of our choices, we discover that it's obedience that frees us from our sins. True happiness is not found in what pleases us. It comes from being at the center of God's love and will. This gives us access to a deeper and richer joy.

Real freedom comes from obeying God, because it guarantees your protection and it positions you to receive His very best.

It moves you from having the mentality of having to "make it happen" to "It's already done." And from "the weight is on my shoulders" to "let's do this together." Your submission to God allows you to enter into a supernatural rest, understanding that your provision and all your needs have been met. Your obedience breaks the back of all forms of bondage that could potentially keep you from reaching your destiny.

God understands that we are not perfect. Sometimes we will miss the mark. Nevertheless, we have Jesus to help us, the Holy Spirit to guide us and the Bible as a light on the way. And that is all we really need!

God longs for us to obey Him, so He can bless us through the plans and purposes He has set for each one of us. Remembering to keep the right perspective of God at heart, will determine our level of trust in God. It's our level of trust that will fuel our obedience. The more fuel we have, the further we can go in life.

I encourage you to let the Holy Spirit show you the areas of your life that need complete or deeper submission to God's will and His word.

Your full potential will only be realized when you make up your mind to fully obey God, no matter what you see in the process.

Your submission will communicate your need for Him and it will make room for more than you could ever imagine. In Ephesians chapter 3, verse 20, it says, "now to him who is able to do immeasurably more than all we ask or imagine, according to his power that is at work within us." God has amazing things for each of us, but it all starts with His power working in tandem with our obedience. God's plans may not always play-out the way you expected, but you can surely trust that His plans are always best. Submit to God wholeheartedly. He truly loves you and has nothing but your best interest at heart. So, let Him in and let Him lead the way.

Resist The Devil

As we decide to obey and follow God, we will encounter a lot of opportunities to compromise our character and abort our faith. We will be faced with many trials and tribulations. No one is exempt from facing challenges. We all have situations that pressure us and tempt us to throw in the towel or do things we shouldn't do. What I have learned over the years though, is that life is more about how you respond, than about what is happening or has happened to you. I know this from having struggles of my own, and I'm sure that you can relate to that.

Naturally speaking, we can have power, talents, resources, and different opportunities that come along, but if we are not under God's authority, we don't really have any relevant authority. As followers of Christ, our power comes from submitting to God. It is through this power that we inherit the earth and become people that God can use for expanding His kingdom.

We only have ruling authority when we are yielded to God's authority and obey Him. The bottom line is that our obedience is a demonstration of love and it comes from reading, meditating, and acting upon the Word of God.

Our ability to resist temptation and overcome hardships will ultimately determine the course of our lives. We must make a quality decision ahead of time about who we are going to be and what we will or will not do, if we intend to overcome temptation. We must be intentional with our standards. Will you fight against it, or will you give in and roll with it?

Now, as we fight against temptation, please keep in mind that there is grace for our shortcomings. There is grace for when we miss the mark. However, abusing God's grace will always lead us to a life of dysfunction and destruction.

When we fall into temptation, we lose opportunities because we are out of position to receive what God has for us. It's like having an umbrella but holding it down at your feet. Will it keep you dry in that position? Of course not! The same is true for us. When we give into temptation repeatedly, we risk our effectiveness and purpose in the earth.

Temptation is tricky because it comes from within. Let me elaborate better with an example. Sex is not bad. It's our desire to have it before marriage that turns it into a temptation that can then lead us to sin and away from God's will for our lives.

The same is true when we commit ourselves to a specific goal like "not eating sugar" for a specific amount of time. Then, we go to a family gathering and see a ginormous chocolate cake on the table. The cake itself is not bad, eating it is not sinful and our families didn't put it there to try and make us break our commitment. The dynamic between us and the cake is being fostered by the temptation that is coming from our own hearts. The battle between what we want and what we know we need happens inside of us.

The Bible says in James chapter 1, verses 13 and 14 that, *"when tempted, no one should say, "God is tempting me."* For God cannot be tempted by evil, nor does He tempt anyone; but each person is tempted when they are dragged away by their own evil desire and enticed."* God does not tempt us and the situations around us don't have the power to force us into sin. We have been given the authority to govern our lives and to decide what we will and will not do. God has given us free will, and we all can live in or out of alignment with God's word. It's a decision!

In 1 Corinthians chapter 10, verse 13, scriptures also mention that *"no temptation has overtaken you except what is common to mankind. And God is faithful; He will not let you be tempted beyond what you can bear. But when you are tempted, He will also provide a way out so that you can endure it."* This means that every time we are tempted, God has already provided a way of escape. So, the question becomes, will you take the way out or be led astray by your own desires?

Truly loving God and being "purpose driven" have been two of the biggest catalysts in helping me overcome temptation. Keeping the big picture in mind makes distractions and temptations seem more miniscule. Focusing on the plan that God has for my life is a full-time job and it leaves little time for foolery and playing games. Temptations are traps sent by the enemy to steal your joy, your time and anything else you will allow him to put his hands on. I have missed the mark many times and have been led astray by my own personal desires, but because I have this foundation, it doesn't throw my life off as much as you could imagine. None of us are perfect, but that doesn't mean we can't be the best that God intended for us.

Because I understand these things and I desperately want to receive everything that God has for me, it makes it easier to resist temptation. I have a made-up mind to follow God, no matter what! I believe that has made the biggest difference in my life. When obeying God is negotiable, you will always find yourself in a compromising situation. You must have a "made up mind" before you are ever tempted. You must have a made-up mind that you are going to follow God's plan for your life and that you are going to receive everything that God has for you before you ever become tempted.

God is light! When we spend time in His presence, it illuminates our path. We need to stay connected to Him to have the proper view of everything around us. He is our source and we were never designed to function without Him. Just like a lamp, it can't produce light without being plugged in. It must be connected to a source of power. No power source, no light!

When someone lives without light or even a dim light, they misplace and lose things, because their vision is compromised. The lack of light makes it easier for them to get hurt, as they could potentially bump into things they can't see.

Living a life without structure and dim light will leave you wandering aimlessly between a bunch of daily dead end and disconnected activities. This is the enemy's subtle strategy for unraveling your life. Darkness creates a perfect atmosphere for the enemy to come in and steal from you. The only way to prevent this is to resist Him and turn on a light! Submit to God's Word and allow it to illuminate your destiny.

Song of Solomon says in chapter 2, verse 15, *"Catch for us the foxes, the little foxes that ruin the vineyards, our vineyards that are in bloom."* Many times, we believe that it's only the big things that cause chaos and have the capacity to damage our lives, when it's the continuous, unchecked little things that derail our destiny. But if we stay connected to God as our source, those little things will get exposed and lose power, allowing us to accomplish all that God has set before us.

Lack of proper lighting and structure in one's life is the easiest way to fall into temptation. It may not seem to make sense at first. I mean, won't you accomplish a lot if you're focused on a lot? Not really. The fact is, when Jesus is not the center of your focus, it becomes difficult to manage life. But when you keep Him at the center, it enlarges your capacity to see and do more. Keeping God as the center supernaturally enables you to resist not only temptation but distractions. It helps you keep things in proper perspective.

At the core, when people make a habit of living a life without light and structure, it's because deep down, they don't see themselves as victorious. They don't see themselves winning. They suffer from a lowly self-image. They have goals, but they may not truly believe they can achieve them. They know what the Word of God says but haven't made it the highest truth for their life. When you live life out of focus, it will always leave room for destruction and for distractions to come in and lead you astray.

The enemy uses our lack of focus and low self-esteem to come in and steal the very things we spend time praying for. He tempts us by making us feel like we are not who God says we are. He leads us into thinking we are missing something that God has already promised or provided for us.

The enemy tempted Jesus in Matthew chapter 4, verse 2 saying, *"if you are the Son of God, tell these stones to become bread,"* but Jesus knew better! He didn't have to prove his sonship because He already knew who He was. And neither do you. When you put your faith in Jesus, you are adopted into the royal family of God and therefore become His son or daughter. You gain access to all the promises of God for your life. And everything that belongs to Him belongs to you. You have access to everything pertaining to life and Godliness. You are made victorious! All your battles were won on the cross. You are more than a conqueror in Christ. When you understand this, no temptation will be able to overtake you.

The more you resist temptation, the stronger you become, and the enemy will have less room to get into your life. As a result, the enemy will work harder to sabotage you. His strategies become subtler in hopes they will go on undetected. One of the ways I have seen this play out in my life and the lives of those I have ministered to or coached, is that the enemy tries to tempt us with the areas of our lives that God has already delivered us from. He brings back old people, patterns or behaviors. He tries to torment us with our past mistakes and failures so that we forget the goodness of God and feel tempted to give up. He puts negative memories on replay to keep us contained in our own mind.

But stay strong and remember that *"if God is for you, who can be against you?" (Romans 8:31)* He delivered us and therefore we have everything we need to move forward and to stay on track. We must "put on the full armor of God" (Ephesians 6:10-18) each day and decide to obey away. As we make up our mind to trust and follow God, we can be sure to rise above the temptation.

The Bible says in James chapter 4, verse 7, *"Submit yourselves, then, to God. Resist the devil, and he will flee from you."*

Many people read this scripture and focus only on resisting the devil, so he will flee. But the most important part of the scripture is submission to God's will and His way of doing things. It's our submission to God that gives us the authority and the power to resist the devil in the first place. Without submission, we can't resist him effectively.

As we engage in the process of obeying away and overcoming temptation again and again, the easier it will become to stay committed to God's plans and purposes. Resisting temptation becomes easier because just like a muscle it develops memory. Take courage and continue fighting the good fight of faith.

Start, Stop and Continue!

When it comes to obedience, this is how I think about it. Most of the time our obedience will fall into one or more of these three categories: start, stop or continue. God will either lead you to start doing something, stop doing something or continue to do something as a way of obeying Him.

Starting implies that you will begin something entirely new. It requires stepping out in faith and taking action that you may or may not feel ready to do. Stopping on the other hand, is more disruptive and it requires more self-control and discipline. It demands that you choose Christ over your comfort zone. It provokes you to give up your way to receive God's will. Continuing requires you to persevere and to be consistent with behaviors that are already in motion. All are easier said than done and the each present their own set of challenges.

Personally, I feel like starting and continuing are usually a lot easier for me than stopping. I think it's because sometimes I am so focused on what I should start doing next that I overlook the things I need to stop doing to move forward. It's like I put the cart before the horse.

Let me explain better with an example. Over the years, I have struggled on and off with my sleeping schedule, whether it's going to bed on time or getting up early. I used to think my issue was the getting up early part, but I recently discovered that the problem I experience in the mornings, when my alarm clock goes off a million times, and I decide to push snooze because I'm exhausted, all comes from staying up too late the night before. So, to start getting up earlier to be more efficient during the day, I first need to stop going to bed so late.

I usually have two "excuses" for staying up late. Number one, I convince myself that, "I need to stay up late to finish something important," when most times it could wait until the next morning or it could have been done hours before if I had properly managed my time during the day. Number two, I tell myself, "I worked so hard today, I deserve to stay up late and do whatever I want to do," so I end up doing things like talking on the phone, cleaning out my closet, making snacks, or researching random beauty tips, when I should be in bed seconds away from sleeping.

As a business woman, I have come to realize that neither one of these excuses serve me well, and in fact they both work against my destiny and calling. Resting well is essential for me to be able to carry out all my daily duties and for me to operate at peak performance. I know for a fact that I will not always be able to sleep eight hours per night, but as I make a practice of stopping to start, it allows me to reach a place of balance, where I have the energy to fuel my daily routine.

So, you see, many times our start is dependent upon our stop. We must be willing to make the proper adjustments to align our lives with not only our truth but "the" truth of God's Word and His ways if we want to reap the benefits of living a Christian life.

God taught me a lot about the importance of start, stop and continue within the principle of obeying away when He started to refine me as a leader.

As I mentioned before, I am a social butterfly and I love hanging out with friends and talking. But, as I matured and grew in my relationship with Christ, the Holy Spirit started to show me how and when to obey away from certain conversations. He also showed me when to start talking and when I should stop and just be silent. There were moments when He simply wanted me to step away from certain conversations or cut communication with certain people. Not because they were bad, or the conversations were bad, but because they were just not good for me.

Not everything God asks you to obey away from is bad. It might not just be good for you. It's not our job to call that shot. Our job is to have faith that God knows best and simply listen for His voice and then do what He says.

When I first realized what God was prompting me to do, I didn't think it was a big deal and I felt like God was being overprotective. After all I really enjoyed socializing, and how harmful could one conversation be? After a while of being disobedient God began to deal with me in a more intentional way. I would be in the middle of telling a story or listening to someone else speak and I would hear the Lord saying, "Ok Ashley, enough, stop or walk away!"

His voice would become so loud in my ear that it was impossible for me to ignore. I later discovered through His revealing of situations and circumstances that He was protecting me from being in situations that would damage me or could even potentially jeopardize my growth.

Obedience does not require our opinions or preferences, but it does require us to trust God. It works best when we don't stop to question God, but rather respond quickly to His instructions. Delayed obedience is still disobedience. You start to play Russian Roulette with your future when you refuse to obey away.

Obedience to God is a long-life process of start, stop and continue! If there are areas of your life where you still don't have results, or you still need a breakthrough, ask yourself "Am I obeying God? Have a done the last thing he's told me to do?"

Once you get the answers to these questions, make the necessary adjustments and God will honor you for it. He will always illuminate the path you need to take. He loves you and

He never wants you to be confused about His will for your life. If you ask for it, He will always give you the wisdom to know what to start, stop and continue.

CHAPTER 10

INCREASE YOUR CAPACITY

When I am coaching clients, I often say, "everyone thinks they are a champion, until they spend a day with one." The reality is that anytime we think we have it all figured out, chances are that we have no idea.

I know this to be true in my own life. There have been several times when I've underestimated the level of effort and sacrifice that a specific achievement took, or the amount of discipline and perseverance required for a successful person to acquire and maintain optimal results. It was only the grace of God that allowed me to see up close the undergoing decisions and moves that certain leaders around me make to accomplish their goals. This allowed me to understand what to do or what not to do when it was my turn. Without these type of moments and associations, who knows what other mistakes I would have made in life.

Not all of us have had good examples to follow or mentors to show us the way. We haven't all had people who can help us transition from the pits to the palaces of life. The problem with our limited information is that when we don't have a revelation of what it takes to achieve our goals or receive our heart's desires, it is easy to be deceived and become unrealistic about what the outcomes of our efforts should be. On the other hand, when we do get the revelation of what it takes, it can feel intimidating and cause us to shut down, stop acting, or lose hope.

There is so much involved in the process of succeeding in life. We can't sum it all up with what we see on stage. Most of the work is done behind the scenes. Many love the idea of being in the spotlight and being on platforms, but most are unwilling to make the necessary sacrifices and put in the work required to get there.

It's just like going to school, you can't go from one grade to the next without meeting the prerequisites for that next level. For example, you can't go from 1st grade to 5th grade without finishing the work that's required, right? Or turn in 2nd grade homework all year and graduate from 8th grade. It doesn't work that way. There are prerequisites that must be met for you to pass through to the next level. I think a lot of times we are trying to get God to give us the benefits that come with that next dimension or that next level in our career, in our relationships, in our businesses, but we haven't graduated from our current level. Or we feel like, "Hello? Are you listening? I'm ready now God, you should promote me now!" but we haven't met his prerequisites.

There is always a "behind the scenes" process and prerequisites to meet before we can break free to each new dimension of our lives. There are sacrifices that must be made and challenges that we need to face.

There is a price to pay for greatness and no one is exempt from paying it.

It's just like when you're driving, after a certain number of miles, depending on where you live, you'll be met with a toll to pay. If you want to continue traveling onto the next section of that road, you must pay it. There will always be a price to pay to reach your final destination. The question is, are you willing to pay it?

In the last chapter, we talked about the airport security checkpoint, remember? We used it as an example to elaborate on the process of reaching your "final destination" for your destiny in life. We talked about leaving your emotional baggage on the ground so that you can "fly."

Well, when passing through that same security checkpoint, not only does it require that our bags get checked so that we can move forward, it also requires us to have a valid ticket. Only the people who paid the price for the flight will be permitted on the plane. Everyone else must stay on the ground. If you don't pay the price, you can't board the plane. It's really that simple. Although salvation is free, a gift we receive by faith, there are prerequisites to inherit the promises of God.

Private and Public Self

What we do privately is what nurtures our results publicly. You can't compare your backstage to what you see happening on other people's opening night. Simply work on you! The Bible tells us that it is not wise to compare ourselves with others.

In Galatians 6, verses 4 to 5 says that; each one should test their own actions. Then they can take pride in themselves alone, without comparing themselves to someone else, for each one should carry their own load.

Comparing yourself to others will always lead to confusion and discouragement. We should all be focused on and concerned with our own progress and growth. Now, I don't mean that we should be selfish and neglect or overlook people in their processes, we can all contribute to each other's success. However, it is important that we intentionally understand and are honest with ourselves about what areas of our life need attention and correction if we are truly going to break free.

Our life is a race! And although it may look like we all begin from the same position visually, we are not. We all have different starting points depending on our background, experiences, skill level, associations, and so on. Our conditions are all different. You can't run the race comparing your performance to those around you because we all have different advantages and disadvantages. You must simply focus on your own journey, looking forward, staying strong, and crossing the finish line.

Comparing yourself to those around you is dangerous because it stunts your growth spiritually and mentally. The feelings of "not adding up" or "being enough" can overwhelm you to a point that you stop taking action. The pain of comparison is emotionally paralyzing. It literally tries to stop you from moving forward. How can you finish a race, if you don't run? Comparison cultivates a spirit of "imitation" instead of authenticity. Its goal is to make you lose yourself in the admiration of someone else.

In Matthew 25, verses 14 to 30, Jesus shares *The Parable of the Bags of Gold*. In other versions of the Bible, the gold is presented as talents, this is important, so we know that this parable applies to all kinds of resources God places in our hands, whether they are financial resources, skills and opportunities, or spiritual gifting's.

So, God gives some bags of gold to three of his servants. In verse 15 it says that to each one, he gives different amounts, according to his ability. This is crucial to the story, because many times we compare ourselves to each other and resent God for not giving us enough money or skills, enough connections, or opportunities. God gives to each one of us, exactly what we need and what he already knows we can handle. He gives us different things to work with, depending on the purpose he has set for each one of us.

Different jobs, different callings, and different experiences. So, although the amounts were not equal, they were fair. **To each one he gave an opportunity.**

The question is not how is your neighbor going to play his deck of cards, but how are you going to play yours. What are you going to do with your skills and talents, with your opportunities, with your money, and with your challenges?

It is important to also understand that God expects us to harvest fruit from whatever he places in our hands, but those expectations manifest accordingly to what he has given us. Notice that he didn't reply differently to the servant that brought a five-bag return and the one that brought a two-bag return. But he did react differently to the one that hid the money and did nothing.

God is merciful, and he gives us all something to work with. So, let's work that thing! Work your business! Work that marriage! Work that gift! Work that dream! Let's be careful not to end up like the third servant that lost what he was given, simply because he was too afraid to step out on faith and work that thing.

As the body of Christ, we all have different callings, but none of these callings make us different in value before God. An eye can't lift things up and a hand can't see which path is best to take. The best thing for you to do, is be the best with finding and fulfilling your purpose. Don't compare, don't complain, just embrace your original design and propel.

When it comes to our personal and professional growth, comparing is always a bad idea. However, if we notice that there are areas of ourselves or of our lives that seem underdeveloped or damaged, we should ask God to heal us and help us become whole. God is always willing and ready to help us, when we open our hearts to him and ask. The place where I have seen people get messed up the most is when they put all the responsibility on God. Waiting on God means we trust him to come through for us, but it doesn't mean we shouldn't take ownership or do our part. A lot of times we misinterpret our role and God's role in the equation.

For example, you may be praying for God to bring you into debt free status, but when he blesses you with an idea to make money you decide not to move out on it because of fear. Perhaps God blesses you with the resources to pay your bills, but instead you spend the money on other stuff like traveling or buying clothes. My point in saying all of this is simple. **God specializes in the impossible, but it's our job to do the possible**. Once he reveals the areas of our character and life that need attention, we should always pray but we must also take action.

We can't be passive or irresponsible about our spiritual and emotional development. We are all responsible for making sure that we are taking the right steps and making the right decisions to grow. Confronting ourselves and taking ownership for where we are in life can be challenging and nerve racking. It takes courage. But as I have said and heard many others say; well, if it was easy, then everyone would be doing it. Doing the private, "inside" work is never easy, but it will always be worth it.

Let me illustrate this further, because I believe this is one of the areas that can make or break the life of a believer. Floyd Mayweather is a world class boxer. He is extremely gifted. When people see him fight, they are enamored by his level of skill and strength. It is clear to see while he is fighting that it's challenging, but because he is so talented and practiced, he makes it look easy. The truth is that his boxing performance is only the result of his private training. All the hard work, dedication, and sacrifices he made in his personal time, behind the scenes.

There are no shortcuts to success.

How you practice privately will determine how your life plays out publicly.

My pastor gives this one illustration in a lot of his messages and it makes me think of this very idea. Back in the day, he was a pilot. He often describes how when you are going up in altitude while flying, you can feel the turbulence start to hit the plane. As the pilot, you must be listening to the people on the ground floor for instructions on what adjustments to make so that you can fly above it. So, on the way up, you are listening and making constant corrections to make it to that smooth place in the sky.

This illustration parallels our break free journey perfectly and I believe this is how many of us try to operate. Except, sometimes we make just enough corrections to survive the turbulence, but not enough to rise above it.

What corrections is God asking you to make in your life, so that you can make it to that smooth place? I'm not saying that once you get there, everything will be perfect, but I'm sure that there is something in your life that you would like to be better. You may never have the opportunity to be around a professional athlete champion and you may never fly a plane, but we all have opportunities to grow, and to succeed. You may not even have the natural examples around you, like a mother or a mentor, but God can be that example if you let him. His word will train you for the fights of life and he will help you rise above its challenges and win.

Don't Assume, Ask Questions

Having someone to learn from is always a good starting point. But you also need to learn how to ask the right questions. It is only by asking the right questions, that we can get the knowledge we need to go to the next season of our lives.

We need to fearlessly ask ourselves the tough questions. Jesus didn't die for us to be mediocre and to live an average life. After all, if your life is anything less than God's best, what would make you different from anyone else living in the world? Nothing right?

As children of God, we are called to stand out. We are set apart (Deuteronomy 14:2). Our lives should not be so basic that they go unnoticed, blending in with the rest of the world. I encourage you to reflect on your character and all other areas of your life to see if the results you have; match what God has promised you.

The Bible says in Psalm chapter 112, verse 3 that wealth and riches are in their houses, and their righteousness endures forever. There are many things that God promises us in the Bible, not just wealth and riches, in Deuteronomy 6, verses 10 to 12, Moses talks to the people from Israel and says: *When the Lord your God brings you into the land he swore to your fathers, to Abraham, Isaac and Jacob, to give you—a land with large, flourishing cities you did not build, houses filled with all kinds of good things you did not provide, wells you did not dig, and vineyards and olive groves you did not plant—then when you eat and are satisfied, be careful that you do not forget the Lord, who brought you out of Egypt, out of the land of slavery.*

A lot of getting the right results, in life, business, relationships, comes from asking yourself and God the right questions.

God wants to guide us and show us what he has for us. But we need to be willing to ask him what he wants us to do, and then put his response into motion.

The issue here is that many times we are tempted to look outside of ourselves for both the problem and the solution, when most of the time, we can find them living in our own hearts. It is easy to get caught up in the blame game that can cause you to judge the process of others and point the finger without ever doing any self-reflection.

Check for everything! Check to see if you have the fruit of the Holy Spirit; love, joy, peace, patience, kindness, goodness, faithfulness, gentleness, and self-control. Do you see evidence of God's grace and promises in your relationships, in your job, in your character, and/or in your finances? Let's be clear, I understand that we are all works in progress. You might be working on developing some of these attributes in your life right now, but it you have been a Christian for several years and you don't see God's word blossoming and becoming a daily reality in your life, you should start to ask yourself some questions.

Many times, we don't get the answers we need or get delivered out of challenging situations because we are unwilling to ask God or ourselves the right questions. This could happen for several reasons:

Fear of what the answer will be.

The fear of confronting ourselves.

Insecurity or uncertainty about what questions to ask.

Breakthrough most often begins by asking the right questions.

We may not always get the most comfortable answer, but we will always get the most accurate and beneficial one.

There is this story in the Bible, in 2 Kings 4, where a woman shared her worries with a very well-known prophet in her town:

-Your servant my, husband is dead, and you know that he

revered the Lord. But now his creditor is coming to take my two boys as his slaves.

Elisha replied to her:

How can I help you? Tell me, what do you have in your house?

To what she replied:

-Your servant has nothing there at all, she said, except a small jar of olive oil.

Elisha then told her:

-Go around and ask all your neighbors for empty jars. Don't ask for just a few. Then go inside and shut the door behind you and your sons. Pour oil into all the jars, and as each is filled, put it to one side.

She obeyed, and was marveled at how each one of the jars was filled. So much so, that the bible says it would be enough to pay her debts and live on what was left.

Many times, we miss out on what God has for us, simply because we are unable to identify what we already have to succeed in life. We don't recognize what we already have in us and around us to start walking with God and to experience the miraculous. Are you able to recognize this in your own life? How much more can God do with whatever you have your right now? In your house? In your marriage? In your business?

Make sure not to surround yourself with pushovers that are passive about your destiny, but with people that will lovingly challenge your comfort zone. People that will ask you tough questions that unlock your full potential and release God's plans and purposes for your life.

Questions like "do you want to be healed?" Or "what do you have in your house?", are powerful because they make you investigate the condition of your heart and challenge your perspective. That, many times, is all God needs to start working in your life.

Seek for God, and expect the results. If you're not getting results, dare to ask God the hard questions.

I use working out as a very recurrent example because a lot of people can relate to it. So, here it is one last time. If you're adjusting in your daily routine but you're still not losing weight, you should be asking some questions.

Are your adjustments the right ones? Are you being diligent and disciplined enough? Do you need more support?

The problem is that many of us become discouraged before we ever question our strategy. Discouragement is dangerous, as it can lead to false contentment, complacency, and finally to complaining. This gets you down and you will end up losing focus. Understand that opposition will come, but keep your joy!

Don't allow discouragement to stop you from being curious. Ask away! God will reveal everything you need to know to move forward. He wants you to break free. Take one step at a time and continue to trust God along the way.

Capacity for Change

Every time God pushes me into the next dimension of my life, he requires me to change. Change is good, but it can also be terrifying.

In many of those moments, I felt like saying to him:

-You know God, I think we've done enough so far. I am okay with this level of impact and influence. It would be perfectly fine for me if I just stay right here.

I have had to change many times, and truth be told, I will never stop changing. If you want to live out the fullness of the plans and purpose of God, neither will you. We are all works in progress until we meet with Jesus. Some changes are easier than others, but nevertheless, I have to make the proper adjustments to my life. **Every point of increase will require you to change.**

The Bible says in Hebrews 13 verse 8 that God changes not, it says: *Jesus Christ is the same yesterday and today and forever.*

So, whatever He said he is going to do, He will do it! God has already given us everything we need to live a good life and on top of that He has already promised us success and victory.

The Bible proves this to us repeatedly. Let's read a couple of verses to better illustrate this point:

2 Peter 1:3 New Living Translation (NIV)
His divine power has given us everything we need for a godly life through our knowledge of him who called us by his own glory and goodness.

2 Corinthians 2:14 New Living Translation (NIV)
But thanks be to God, who always leads us as captives in Christ's triumphal procession and uses us to spread the aroma of the knowledge of him everywhere.

John 10:10 New Living Translation (NIV)
The thief comes only to steal and kill and destroy; I have come that they may have life, and have it to the full. (NLT says rich and satisfying life).

We could spend all day discovering scriptures that promise us a glorious life. The promises of God are available to us since the beginning of time, before we were even born. Jesus already did, on the cross, everything that he needed to do pertaining to our lives. We are victorious in his name! But, we still need to act to embrace those promises and allow them to impact and transform our lives.

We need to stop praying as if God has a limited number of blessings to give per day. There are no shortages in heaven. No shortages of resources, blessings or anything. But still, know that God is wise and loving, sometimes his answer is no.

So, the question you need to ask is:

-Why are so many of us walking around without what he promised us in our lives?

It is simple; the problem lays here on earth with our ability to receive what is coming from the sender.

Many times, we think we are ready for what God has, and we want him to fill us up with his best. For example, maybe we want more members in our church, more employees in our business, maybe we want a spouse and children, to increase our income, or move into a bigger house.

Whatever the case might be, we first need to ask ourselves if we have enough space to hold it? Is there enough room in our hearts? Do we have the intellectual capacity for it? The emotional capacity? Many times, after honestly asking ourselves these questions, we will realize that we are already too full to receive anything more. We are filled up with old spiritual patterns, traditions, unhealthy behavior, unforgiveness, broken relationships, and emotional baggage; which leaves us with no space for God to deposit anything else into us.

Sometimes there are things that God wants to do in us, through us and for us but we are in the way. Our lack of spiritual maturity, fears, and insecurities are blocking whatever he wants to accomplish. I realize that this is not everyone's story. There are seasons where we have done all that we can do, and we simply must wait on the Lord. However, when you notice a pattern, it is always good to pray and crack the code.

In my personal life, whenever I notice things are going too slow or I experience stagnation, many times the common denominator is me. I am the one that needs to change, stretch, grow, evolve, and develop. I have learned that in seasons like this, the best strategy is to humble myself and ask God to help me change. We can't change ourselves. We need God to change us!

In Isaiah 54, verse 2, God talks to his people, the Israelites. Through our faith in Jesus, we are all part of God's holy nation, which means we are also being told these same words: *"Enlarge the place of your tent, stretch your tent curtains wide, do not hold back; lengthen your cords, strengthen your stakes."*

Notice the keywords in the scripture, enlarge, stretch, lengthen, and strengthen.

When I studied these words out a bit more I discovered that they meant -grow large, to go beyond, to make more room, to break out, to breakthrough, to expand, go further, occupy new territories, no limits, no boundaries, thinking big-. Bottom line, "increase capacity."

There is that word again; "capacity."

As you are reading or listening to this book you might be wondering:

-Why is it so important for me to increase my capacity?

Well, this is how I see it. If you only have enough joy, peace, provision, or whatever the case might be for yourself, then you simply don't have enough. God wants us to have more than enough so that we can be a blessing to others. He wants us to be in a position where we can freely give to those around us.

The whole earth is waiting for you to move in signs, wonders, and miracles. They are waiting on you to change things, but we can't change anything in the world unless we are first changed by God. **Changing the world requires power and power requires capacity.**

Being a blessing to others is not about us getting recognition, but about God's glory being revealed on earth. God set everything up so that we can be a gift to the world. But nobody gives a gift that is not ready to be unwrapped or "revealed." God wants us to be the best example of his goodness, of his love, of his grace once he reveals us to the world.

Many times, we are asking God for more, but we don't have enough room to receive in:

Our heart
Our emotions
Our intellect
Our character
Our imagination
Our schedules

I don't know what you are asking God to give you more of; it could be more friends, more income, or more opportunities. Or maybe a bigger ministry, a better job, a marriage. But the question you should be asking yourself is:

-Do I have enough capacity to hold it?

There are no limits around us, only the ones that exist within us.

It is super important that we allow ourselves to grow and be stretched. So that we can go to the next level: in our relationships, in our businesses, in our friendships, in our marriages, in our schooling, in our careers, in our gifting, and graced places.

Whenever we lack the capacity that God needs to move, the supernatural stops. Remember when we talked about the woman with the jars? There was so much to learn from this story.

Praise the Lord, this woman got her family out of debt, because she followed the man of God's instructions. Her obedience led to her breakthrough. God's blessing flowed in supernatural ways, and the oil continue to pour out until there were no more jars to fill. However, notice that the oil stopped multiplying when she no longer had the capacity to capture it! If she had more jars, meaning "more capacity to receive", the oil would have continued pouring out and maybe she could have paid the debts of everyone in her community or at least on her block.

When our capacity is limited, the supernatural stops.

Another good example is when Peter went fishing. This story is in Luke 5, verses 1 to 7:

One day as Jesus was standing by the Lake of Gennesaret, the people were crowding around him and listening to the word of God. 2 He saw at the water's edge two boats, left there by the fishermen, who were washing their nets. 3 He got into one of the boats, the one belonging to Simon, and asked him to put out a little from shore. Then he sat down and taught the people from the boat. 4 When he had finished speaking, he said to Simon, "Put out into deep water, and let down the nets for a catch." 5 Simon answered, "Master, we've worked hard all night and haven't caught anything. But because you say so, I will let down the nets." 6 When they had done so, they caught such a large number of fish that their nets began to break. 7 So they signaled their partners in the other boat to come and help them, and they came and filled both boats so full that they began to sink.

Peter's obedience blessed not only him, but also his partners. They weren't even working hard, but they benefited because of their association to him. Peter's nets alone would not get the job done, he had to call in for backup. He had to increase his capacity to receive more, but he also had to increase his capacity to believe God. That is the real miracle. When Peter decided to believe and try again, even though he failed previously, it sparked the supernatural.

Let's dig a little bit deeper into the story and hopefully you'll be able to make an even more personal connection.

Question:

-Why didn't Jesus just show up and tell Peter to catch some fish, grab some lemon pepper seasoning and simply have a fish fry?

Answer:

-He knew that Peter's faith needed to grow so he taught him first to increase his capacity to believe. If Jesus had walked up and just said, cast your nets and catch some fish, Peter would have probably looked at Jesus like he was crazy and kept it moving.

Question:

-Did Jesus make the fish appear?

Answer:

-No, the fish were there all the time. Peter just had to have his capacity to understand increased. Peter had to change his perception.

Have you ever heard this before? Perception is Reality.

It's true!

When we perceive the right things, our capacity to receive is right and it puts us in a position to receive everything that God wants to do in us, through us and around us.

Although this may not always be the case, I think many times we underestimate God's ability to provide in our life. As a result, we may not properly prepare ourselves like we should to receive what he has already promised us. For example, if you believe that it's God's desire for you to be wealthy, you would prepare yourself to learn more about money management, investments and stewardship as a general principle.

Or if you believe that God is going to send you a spouse, maybe you would begin learning about unconditional love and or how to engage into a healthy relationship. In many ways, I believe a person's level of preparation reveals their level of belief. Let me give you some examples, you can't say you are preparing to entertain guests in your home, if you are laying around in your pajamas with no food in the fridge. It just doesn't make sense. You can't walk around talking about how your business is about to explode and how you are expecting more clients, if you haven't taken the time to build the strategy, structure or systems to serve them.

If you believe that it's possible, you will prepare for it.

Those two biblical stories are great examples of what happens when we increase our capacity to believe and understand.

Capacity Is Void

God is a gap-filler. He is masterful at filling voids. But how can you fill someone that is already full? How do you get a pregnant woman pregnant, that's already pregnant?

Increasing our capacity is a digging down and digging out process. It requires a removal of anything that could potentially hinder or damage the plans and purposes that God has for our life. If we want to receive God's best, it is necessary for us to make the proper adjustments. I think sometimes we try to avoid the "void" because that "making room" process can be painful. Being stretched and strengthened is uncomfortable and it hurts.

It is easy to rejoice over resurrection, but can we endure the cross? The Bible says in second Corinthians, chapter 1, verse 7, *"And our hope for you is firm, because we know that just as you share in our sufferings, so also you share in our comfort."* Meaning that living a life with God includes comfort, but it also includes hardships and sufferings. It challenges our comfort zone and the way things have always been. Increasing our capacity is a chiseling, breaking down to breakthrough process that includes removing the old to make space for the new or to make room for more.

It is like making space in soil to plant a new seed. If you simply put the seed on top of the soil, it will not grow. You must dig deep into the soil and create space for the seed to be planted and eventually with proper care and attention it will grow. A tree will never grow taller than its roots can sustain.

Or think about what happens on a construction site when they are ready to build a new resort or to expand a property. They use a wrecking ball to destroy whatever was there before to create the capacity for what they want to build next.

In Genesis chapter 1, God formed the earth in 6 days and then he filled it. In the beginning God created the heavens and the earth. Subsequently, God called light into the world and separated the waters to form the sky and the dry land. Then he added vegetation, living creatures, and birds. And finally, in Genesis chapter 2, verse 7, the Bible says; *God formed a man from the dust of the ground and breathed into his nostrils the breath of life, and the man became a living being.* Everything God forms, he fills.

So, we don't have to worry about trying to find ways to fill ourselves up when we fill empty. For example, filling ourselves with food when we feel lonely. Or buying clothes we can't afford to reinforce our identity. Or compromising our values to win the attention of the opposite sex because we're tired of being single.

There are so many examples in the Bible of people experiencing this "digging down" process or "void" to be filled with more of what God wanted to do in their lives and in those around them. In all these examples, there is what I like to call a "capacity move." Essentially an action or paradigm shift that required exceptional faith. If I added every story that supports this understanding, this book would never end. So, I chose two examples that I thought seemed most relatable.

First, let's talk about Abraham. God asked him to leave everything behind to pursue his purpose. God promised Abraham that He was going to bless him and make his name great. He was required to leave everything old and familiar to make space for the new.

The Lord had said to Abram, *"Go from your country, your people and your father's household to the land I will show you"*

2 *"I will make you into a great nation,*
 and I will bless you;
 I will make your name great,
 and you will be a blessing.
 (Genesis 12:1 – 2).

I can't imagine how hard this must have been. I mean, he didn't even know where he was going. The only thing Abraham had was God's instruction. To this day, his capacity move carries a huge impact in our lives. This is a great example of that digging in and digging out process I talked about earlier. Abraham's story is a great example of how we can exercise our faith to create room for what God wants to do in our life.

Now, we talked about Gideon already, but he is such a great example of the message I would like you to understand. The mighty warrior who was referenced in chapter 4. His story is so inspiring and shows us how God pushes us and challenges us in order to develop into the champions that we were meant to be.

What Cripples Our Capacity?

There are many things that try to cripple our capacity as we reach for new levels in our lives. The more aware we are of these barriers the better chance we have of defeating them.

Remember when we talked about the definition of "increasing capacity?"

To grow large, to go beyond, to make more room, to break out, to breakthrough, to expand, go further, occupy new territories, no limits, no boundaries, thinking big.

Well, to do any of that, we must pay close attention to the things that can hinder our progress.

Here are some of the things that can cripple our capacity:

-Negative thinking
-Pride
-Lying to self or others
-Insecurities
-Selfishness
-Lack of integrity
-Negative words that have been spoken over your life that you are living in   agreement with
-Disobedience
-Interpreting life events without revelation
-Refusing to heed to wisdom
-Negative conversations
-Resistance to change or correction
-Rehearsing past hurts & situations
-Un-forgiveness & Refusal to "let it go"
-Fear, doubt & unbelief
-Ignorance
-Playing the victim
-Negative associations
-Toxic relationships
-Entertaining relationships that God did not endorse

Fear not if you identify with some of the words on this list or have one or more of those scenarios currently playing out in your life. There is hope!

God is good, and he loves us so much. When we confess our faults and sins he is faithful to forgive us. Real repentance and progress comes from acknowledging our shortcomings and deciding to go in a different direction. It is making the decision that whatever is not fruitful in our lives and does not serve God's way or will, must go.

What Increases Our Capacity?

The truth is that there is no specific rhyme or recipe, because God deals with each one of us differently. However, even though we are all different and are called to different assignments, it is God's desire for each one of us to mature spiritually and prosper. As a result, we must be willing to change, so that our lives can change and ultimately, we can change the world.

To do this, we must enlarge our capacity at three different levels: spirit, soul, and body.

Yes! God absolutely wants us to be spiritually sound. However, he doesn't want us equipped in our spirit and still bound in our soul and body. To receive his best, we must participate in his plan and yield to his guidance.

So, let's unpack what these three areas look like, so that we can have a better understanding of the things that we need to focus on in order for our capacity to increase and so that we can ultimately break free:

Spiritual capacity refers to:
Your Relationship with God
Your Spiritual discipline
(reading, studying and meditating scripture, your prayer time, fasting, praise & worship, giving)

Soul capacity refers to:
Your mind
Your will
Your emotions
Your intellect

Your imagination

Body capacity refers to:
Your health
Your finances
Your relationships
Your social interactions
Your success capacities

Understanding how you are constructed in your spirit, soul and body will help you better navigate the process of increasing your capacity. So that you can unlock your full potential and effectively grow into who God has called you to be.

Here are some of the things that can help you increase your capacity:

-Obedience to God's instruction
-Meditating & confessing the Word
-Giving at a greater level
-Serving your church and others
-Reading to learn and going to school
-Stepping out on faith
-Walking in love
-Mentorship and trusted advisors
-Prayer and praying in the Spirit
-Praise and worship
-Positive associations
-Asking the right questions
-Confronting your comfort zone
-Living in the fear of the Lord
-Being coachable
-Asking God questions
-Listening to God's Word

God has so many amazing plans for your life and hopefully you have already experienced some of them, but there is more. Don't you want to leave the earth knowing that you maxed out your potential? That you did everything that God wanted you to do? That you received everything he had for you?

Let's:
Go beyond what we have always done
Make more room
Break out to breakthrough
Expand
Go further
Occupy new territories
Think bigger
And ultimately... increase our capacity.

To help you bring these principles to life, I created a few worksheets. You can download them for free here: http://breakfreebeunstoppable.com/unlockandunleash

When it comes to increasing your capacity for change, it is important to remember that God loves you and that he is not trying to take the things you love away from you, he is simply trying to get something better to you. He is not trying to hurt you; he is trying to help you. God is on your side and he will never forsake you, even when you feel like you are forgotten.

If you want to enjoy a fruitful, authentic, and genuine relationship with God, allow Him to take charge, follow His lead and maintain a humble and coachable heart.

You can't expect to look at a chocolate cake recipe from Betty Crocker, follow almost all the steps but neglect to put in the correct amount of eggs, and then expect the cake to come out with the same taste and texture.

God works through our personality, gifts, abilities, and creativity but if He says two eggs for the cake, you need to put in only two eggs. If He says - leave that relationship, quit that job, start tithing, get up earlier, spend more time with me, or whatever it is you cannot make up your own variation of his instructions or simply do what you want. Not if you want to break free!

It switches up the outcome when you "Do You". Not only that, but it delays things. I mean, if the texture of the cake does not come out right, you will have to start all over again and that takes more time.

Decide once and for all that you are not going to delay God's promises being fulfilled in your life by trying to formulate your own recipe. He is the top chef of the kitchen we call life.

As you walk with Him, you will start growing and advancing, all the way from Dishwasher to Sous Chef, but there will only be one Top Chef in this kitchen, and it will always be God. If you ever try to outrank Him, you will be mistaken. You are just not cut out for that kind of responsibility, nor do you have the wisdom necessary to do it well. So, let Him take the lead, and learn to tap your feet to His beat and pretty soon all areas of your life will be in sync with His rhythm.

In John 5, there was a dispute about Jesus authority. The Pharisees were disturbed because Jesus was calling God His Father, and in their heads this meant that He was making himself equal with God.

But what Jesus responded lets us know that he was very clear on his role in this relationship:

Jesus gave them this answer, *"Very truly I tell you, the Son can do nothing by himself; he can do only what he sees his Father doing, because whatever the Father does the Son also does" (John 5:19).*

Jesus knew how the relationship with His Father worked. He didn't try His own ideas, He never tried to outrank God. He understood His role in the relationship and played His part perfectly. And by doing so, he showed us how to do it ourselves.

Let's think about God's people for a moment. How many times did God tell the children of Israel not to store up any food while they were in the desert, but instead to believe in Him for their daily provision?

But what happened?

Each day they were trying to do their own thing. They were not coachable, they altered God's recipe, and as a result God left them out there for 40 years and eventually they perished without ever entering the promised land.

Now, as you move forward throughout your journey in life, don't forget your greatest responsibility, to go into the world to share the good news of Jesus (Matthew 28:16-20). This commandment can look very different from one person to the other. Some people will be called to go on a mission to the other side of the world, while some others will be required to stay home and share the gospel with their family and friends, and some others will be given wealth and influence to send workers into the field and to help those in need.

God has something specific for you to do in this earth. And in order for you to do it, you must be transformed, and moved from your comfort zone into the wild adventures of faith.

God is ready for you to break free, not only to your benefit, but for the sake of those around you. You were made to be a light in this world of darkness. So that the love you freely receive, you can freely give.

One good thing to remember is that when God calls us to be a light in the world of darkness, we need to go in fully prepared, and to do that, we must arm ourselves. In Ephesians 6, verses 10 to 18, the Bible says:

10 "Finally, be strong in the Lord and in his mighty power. 11 Put on the full armor of God, so that you can take your stand against the devil's schemes. 12 For our struggle is not against flesh and blood, but against the rulers, against the authorities, against the powers of this dark world and against the spiritual forces of evil in the heavenly realms. 13 Therefore put on the full armor of God, so that when the day of evil comes, you may be able to stand your ground, and after you have done everything, to stand. 14 Stand firm then, with the belt of truth buckled around your waist, with the breastplate of righteousness in place, 15 and with your feet fitted *with the readiness that comes from the gospel of peace. **16** In addition to all this, take up the shield of faith, with which you can extinguish all the flaming arrows of the evil one. **17** Take the helmet of salvation and the sword of the Spirit, which is the word of God. **18** And pray in the Spirit on all occasions with all kinds of prayers and requests. With this in mind, be alert and always keep on praying for all the Lord's people."*

Praise God! This is what's available to you as you continue to press forward. Please remember that God will not dress you; you must put the armor on yourself.

It is a privilege to be loved by such an amazing God. He knows all our flaws and shortcomings, all the things that make us want to disqualify ourselves. Nevertheless, He keeps working in us, He never quits on us. A lot of times we define ourselves with our past and the things that have happened to us, but God only sees our future. When we go from seeing ourselves as failures, and we start to see ourselves as saved sons and daughters, when we can see ourselves through the redemptive work of Christ, all our failures lose power.

You are precious to Him, His beloved, He did everything in his power to save you and keeps pursuing you every day to draw you closer. God is not seeing everything that is wrong about you, he sees everything that is right and your potential in Him. Not because you are perfect or have it all together, but because He is perfect, and *He* has it all together.

Now that we are approaching the end of this book, you need to remember this one important thing. All of these changes will not happen overnight (shout out to all my type "A" personalities). Unlocking your potential and fulfilling your purpose is an ongoing journey and it requires patience.

Although, I do believe that you can speed things up by faith. God is progressive and He is always ready to release his best to you, but He will never skip process! Whatever you need to grow through to break free and become all that He's called you to be, you will have to endure. Don't lose heart though in the in between of life because in due season, God will bring you out!

The Bible reads, *"Let us not become weary in doing good, for at the proper time we will reap a harvest if we do not give up"* (*Galatians 6:9*).

It will not always be popular and it is not easy to decide to become all that God has called you to be, but it will always be worth it. You will be misunderstood and at times mistreated, but count it all joy! Remember that God is fighting for you and that He always has your back. In the times when your hope is deferred, and your strength feels like it's wearing out, remember, everything you need can be found in the Word of God. Read it, meditate on it, and act upon it.

Now, there is one more thing I want to share with you before you leave. Maybe you got this book without knowing what to expect, maybe you got it as a gift, or maybe you bought it expecting a change in your life.

Every chapter in this book was a key to help you unlock your God-given potential. It is my prayer that you would take action, and that this would not just become another book on your shelf. When I say take action, I mean massive action! God is ready to take you on the biggest adventure of your life, but the real question is, are you ready? Are you ready to give up your ways for His will? Your agenda for His action plan? Your pain for His plans and purposes?

God Will Never Stop Pursuing You.

His love never fails and is enough for whatever you need in your life right now. Trust Him.

I pray that you found whatever you were looking for when you decided to pick up this book. Use the keys you were given and unlock your confidence, your business, your book, your marriage, your finances, your faith, your ministry, your health, and your destiny! Whatever is living on the inside of you, waiting for you to give birth.

Remember to be patient with yourself as you take the necessary steps to break free. As my best friend's six-year-old daughter taught me one night over dinner, "patience is good behavior while you wait." So, be gentle with yourself as you daily progress into all that God has called you to be. Oh, and be sure to practice that *good behavior.*

Somedays will be more difficult than others, but don't give up! God's grace is sufficient. If you follow God wholeheartedly, He will always lead you to victory.

Speaking of victory, you did it! You made it to the end of your break free journey! I believe that God is preparing you to move into the next dimension of your life. But, the next part of your break free journey *really* begins after you close this book and decide to make the words on these pages become a reality in your life. What will change? What about you, your relationships, career, business, and thinking will be different after this chapter ends?

I encourage you to take whatever you got from this book and apply it to your life. And to ensure your success, I thought it would be a good idea if we did the same thing here that we did at the end of chapter one — Let's pray!

God, thank You for my life. Thank You for Your unconditional love and the freedom that comes through my relationship with You. Give me the courage to change in any and all areas of my life that are unpleasing to You. Help me to live out my full potential instead of reliving my past. Help me to apply what I have learned in this book so that I can grow into the best version of myself and fulfill my purpose on earth. I count all past sources of my confidence as worthless and put my hope and expectation in you only. Thank You in advance for the victory in every area of my life. In Jesus's name we pray

— AMEN!

You are now free and unstoppable.

YOUR LIFE MATTERS AND THE WHOLE WORLD IS WAITING ON YOUR BREAKTHROUGH

Only God can fill the empty places in your heart. Nothing else will do — trust me, I tried everything! Whatever you are missing in your life right now, can be found in developing a loving relationship with your Heavenly Father, through His Son, Jesus Christ. I am talking about a *real* relationship, not religion, which goes deeper than church attendance or membership. I believe that knowing God is the only way to live an abundant life filled with peace and purpose.

The Bible says in Romans 10:9, *"that if you declare with your mouth, 'Jesus is Lord,' and believe in your heart that God raised him from the dead, you will be saved."*

All you need to do is declare and believe! If you are ready to break free from fear and the things that have been holding you back from living your best life, please say this prayer with me:

God, I believe Jesus is Your Son and that He died to pay for my sins. I believe You raised Him from the dead and that I now have access to grace, forgiveness, and eternal life in His name. From this day forward, I invite you to take over my life and to become the center of everything I think, say, and do. Help me to love You. Help me to trust You. Help me to become all that You have created me to be, in the mighty name of Jesus I pray, Amen!

Yay! You did it! You established your relationship with God! Now, nurture it through prayer, fellowship, and reading your Bible every day. If you draw near to God, He will draw nearer to you. He has an amazing plan for your life and it starts today.

I am so excited about your future. If you want to stay connected, I would love to hear from you!
Please visit: www.breakfreebeunstoppable.com

Made in the USA
Middletown, DE
01 March 2019